RESEARCH METHODOLOGY
IN
LANDSCAPE
ARCHITECTURE

Nik Ismail Azlan

For book orders, email orders@traffordpublishing.com.sg

Most Trafford Singapore titles are also available at major online book retailers.

Printed in Singapore.

ISBN: 978-1-4669-9867-4 (sc)
ISBN: 978-1-4669-9868-1 (e)

Trafford rev. 04/02/2013

Trafford www.traffordpublishing.com.sg
Singapore
toll-free: 800 101 2656 (Singapore)
Fax: 800 101 2656 (Singapore)

CONTENTS

FOREWORD

This book is written to gain an understanding of the nature and utility of research in the field of landscape architecture planning and design process. It focuses on developing the understanding of the research process essential for students in providing a successful landscape architecture research outcome. It involves the introduction and exploration of problems and opportunities of several basic research methods currently employed in landscape architecture research. Emphasis will be on how researchers identify research topics and develop appropriate research methods. It will also introduce analysis and interpretation of research results. With this caveat, the book provides an array of tools, which includes mapping as well as qualitative and quantitative methods, to make inquiry into landscape architecture research topics and to translate research findings into realistic and usable strategies and solutions. The book builds on the foundation of exploring individual interests for a topical study and how to go about conducting research to address these interests.

PREFACE TO THE THIRD EDITION

This book is written to guide students taking research methodology the basic understanding of the subject matter and able to apply the lessons learnt to conduct a simple research. The book will provide the following information:

a. Understand the definitions of research and types of research

b. The basic concepts of research and the terminologies used in everyday application of research methodology will be dealt with in general terms.

c. Identifying research topics in the built environment and other similar social and scientific research areas that is up to date and relevant to current state of affairs.

d. Selecting appropriate issues and problems within the parameters of the study that are related to the research topics that a student is interested in.

e. Using the problem statement, research objectives and research questions to solve the issues and problems.

f. Choosing the appropriate literature review founded by other researchers to strengthen and acknowledge studies similar to ours.

g. Understand and able to apply the various methodologies used in conducting the research.

h. Collecting the data in the field and laboratory and interpreting them based on selected statistical analysis.

i. Analysing the data to answer and provide the correct solution to the issues and problems

j. To recommend and conclude the outcome of the research.

CHAPTER 1
INTRODUCTION

Everywhere, our knowledge is incomplete and problems are waiting to be solved. We address the void in our knowledge and those unresolved problems by asking relevant questions and seeking answers to them. The role of research is to provide a method for obtaining those answers by inquiringly studying the evidence within the parameters of the scientific method. Research is a study and investigation to discover new facts and information to guide decision makings. In the broadest sense of the word, the definition of research includes any gathering of data, information and facts for the advancement of knowledge.

Further meanings of research

According to the American Heritage Dictionary, research is a scholarly or scientific investigation or inquiry. It is a study people use systematically to produce knowledge. It is a study and investigation to discover new facts and information to guide decision makings. It is also a development and the provision of information to solve a certain problem. Research is a systematic observations and investigations designed to provide reliable information about a particular phenomena. Research is the only dependable way to build on what we know and improve what we can do. Every important advance that is discovered or found is based on evidence and data gathered from research.

As per the Merriam-Webster Online Dictionary, the word *research* is derived from the Middle French "*recherche*", which means "to go about seeking".

The research question or problem is approached systematically by gathering, recording, controlling of empirical and critical investigation of phenomena and analyzing data that is of interest to the researcher. It is a way of looking at accumulated facts so that those data become meaningful in the total process of discovering new insights or to confirm the validity of the solutions of unsolved problems. It involves making a discovery about something previously unknown and entails advancing human knowledge. It helps us to understand, explain or predict things that are of interest to us.

Definition of Research

Research is a systematic process of collecting and analyzing information (data) in order to increase our understanding of the phenomenon with which we are concerned or interested. Although this conception of research may seem somewhat remote and academic, many people rely on a truncated form of it each day to solve smaller problems than those resolved by the more elaborate methodology of formal research. It is with formal research, however, that we are concerned in this text.

Definitions of research by various authors

Several definitions of research given here hopefully will help us to understand research better.

It is a careful, systematic, patient study and investigation in some field of knowledge, undertaken to establish facts or principle (Grinnel, 1993). Grinnel further adds: 'research is a structured inquiry that utilizes acceptable scientific methodology to solve problems and created new knowledge that is generally applicable'.

According to Lundberg (1994), research consists of systematic observation, classification and interpretation of data. The main feature of a scientific research lies in the degree of formality, rigorousness, verifiability and general validity.

Burns (1994) defines research as 'a systematic investigation to find answers to a problem'.

Bullmer (1977) states that, 'research is primarily committed to establishing systematic, reliable and valid knowledge about the social world'.

According to Kerlinger (1986), 'scientific research is systematic controlled empirical investigation of propositions about the presumed relationships about various phenomena.'

What Research is not

The word research has been so loosely employed in everyday speech that few people have any idea of its real meaning. Here are a few guidelines as to what research is not; accompanying each guideline is an illustration depicting the popular concept often held about research.

1. Research is not mere information gathering. A fourth-grade child came home from school with this announcement: "Mama, the teacher sent us to the library today to do research, and I learned a lot about function of trees." This child has been given

the idea that research means going to the library to get information or to glean a few facts. This may be information discovery; it may be learning reference skills; but it certainly is not, as the teacher so termed it, research.

2. Research is not mere transportation of facts from one location to another. A student completes a "research paper" on the trees found in the Lake Garden of Taiping. Although the student did, indeed, go through certain activities associated with formal research—compiling tree species, taking photographs, interviewing the staff of Taiping City Council—these activities still do not add up to a true "research" paper. The student missed the essence of research: the interpretation of data. Nowhere in the paper did the student say, in effect. "These facts that I have gathered seem to indicate some interesting data about the trees in Taiping Lake Garden." Nowhere did the student draw conclusions or interpret the facts themselves. The mere compilation of facts presented with reference citations and arranged in a series, no matter how appealingly neat the format, misses genuine research by a hair. A little farther, and this student would have traveled from one world to another: from the world of mere transportation of fact to the world of interpretation of fact. The difference between the two worlds is the distinction between transference of information and genuine research—a distinction that is important to understand.

3. Unfortunately, many students think that looking up a few facts and transferring them to a written paper

with benefit of references constitutes research. Such activity is, of course, more realistically called fact discovery, fact transportation, and/or fact transcription.

4. Research is not a catchword used to get attention. A letter was sent to your home. You open the envelope and pull out its contents. A statement in boldface type commands attention:

> Years of research have produced an effective pesticide for your garden plants.
> Give your garden plants a healthy growth.

The phrase "years of research" catches your attention. The product must be good, you reasoned, because "years of research" have been spent on developing it. You order the product—and what do you get? Pest control detergent! No research, merely the clever use of a catch-word that, indeed, fulfilled its purpose: to catch my attention. "Years of research"—what an attention-getting phrase, yet how misleading!

What Landscape Architecture Research is

It is a process through which we attempt to achieve systematically and with the support of data the answer to a question, the resolution of a problem, or a greater understanding of a phenomenon within a landscape architecture field. Landscape architecture encompasses the analysis, planning, design, management, and stewardship of the natural and built environments. It involves not only creative expression but also a broad understanding of the context of design: ecosystems, cultural frameworks, functional systems, and social dynamics.

5

Researchers in landscape architecture learn how to change the world by re-imagining and re-shaping the landscape to enhance its artistic and functional dimensions, its ecological health, its cultural significance, and its social relevance. Types of projects that utilized these research components include: residential; parks and recreation; monuments; urban design; streetscapes and public spaces; transportation corridors and facilities; gardens and arboreta; security design; hospitality and resorts; institutional; academic campuses; therapeutic gardens; historic preservation and restoration; reclamation; conservation; corporate and commercial; landscape art and earth sculpture; interior landscapes; and more. All this projects involves, designing through readings, referencing, investigating and systematically enquiring the existing knowledge to further advance the design process and new innovation.

Landscape architecture research applies artistic and scientific principles to the research, planning, design and management of both natural and built environments. Landscape architects apply creative and technical skills and scientific, cultural and political knowledge in the planned arrangement of natural and constructed elements on the land with a concern for the stewardship and conservation of natural, constructed and human resources. The resulting environments shall serve useful, aesthetic, safe and enjoyable purposes.

Further to the above responsibilities landscape architects may conduct research for the purposes of landscape preservation, development and enhancement, include: investigation, selection, and allocation of land and water resources for appropriate use; feasibility studies; formulation of graphic and written criteria to govern the planning and design of land construction programs;

preparation, review, and analysis of master plans for land use and development; production of overall site plans, landscape grading and landscape drainage plans, irrigation plans, planting plans, and construction details; specifications; cost estimates and reports for land development; collaboration in the design of roads, bridges, and structures with respect to the functional and aesthetic requirements of the areas on which they are to be placed; negotiation and arrangement for execution of land area projects; field observation and inspection of land area construction, restoration, and maintenance.

Therefore, landscape architecture research covers a wide variety of topics and can be conducted in several multi-disciplinary areas. It has both ecological and design concerns that included resources for science, art, and also resources that are cross-disciplinary. Examples are three broad areas that are important for critical investigation: urban resources, natural resources, and cultural and human resources. Specific subfields within these areas include: urban design, plant community design; preservation, management and ecological restoration; cultural resource preservation and landscape history; visual resource quality assessment, management and policy; environment-behavior studies; land information systems, policies, applications and management; and design-planning theory and methods.

As the scope of landscape architecture expands to engage with other disciplines, and streams of information directing this field continue to grow and diversify, it becomes increasingly important for landscape architects to be able to implement a range of effective research strategies when seeking, creating, and validating knowledge.

CHAPTER 2

CHARACTERISTICS OF LANDSCAPE ARCHITECTURE RESEARCH

1. Landscape architecture research originates with a question or problem. The landscape architecture world is filled with unanswered questions, unresolved problems. Everywhere we look, we observe things that cause us to wonder, to speculate, to ask questions. And by asking questions, we strike the first spark igniting a chain reaction that terminates in the research process. An inquisitive mind is the beginning of research. There is so much that we do not know that we do not understand! The hope of mitigating our ignorance lies in the questions we ask and the information we gather and in whose collective meaning we may find insight.

Look around you. Consider the unresolved situations that evoke these questions: Why? What's the cause of that? What does it all mean? These are everyday questions. With questions like these, research begins.

2. Research requires a clear articulation of a goal. A clear, unambiguous statement of the problem is critical. This statement is an exercise in intellectual honesty. It cannot brook vagueness, washing, or the avoidance of an obligation to set forth clearly and in a grammatically

complete sentence precisely what the ultimate goal of the research is. The statement asks the researcher, "What precisely do you intend to do?" This is basic and is required for the success of any research undertaking. Without it, the research is on shaky ground indeed.

3. Research requires a specific plan of procedure. Research is not an excursion into happy expectation, of fondly hoping that the data necessary to solve the problem will somehow fortuitously turn up. It is, instead, a carefully planned attack, a search-and-discover mission explicitly planned in advance. Consider the title of a text by Leedy: Practical Research: Planning and Design. The last three words are the important ones. The overall research effort must be explicitly planned and logically designed. Researchers plan their overall research design and specific research methods in a purposeful way—that is, to yield data relevant to their particular research problem. Depending on the specific research question, different designs and methods will be more or less appropriate.

In section 2 of this research characteristics, you considered the goal for research; that was what you intended to do. Here, you state the plan, the design; this is how you propose to reach that goal. You must not wait until you're chin deep in the project to plan and design your strategy; In the formative stages of the research project, much can be decided: Where are the data? Do any existent data address themselves to the research problem? Even if the data exist, is it reasonable that you have access to them? Presuming that you have access to the data, what will you do with them after they are in your possession? I might go on and on. These questions merely hint that planning and design cannot be postponed. Each of the questions above must have an answer early in the research process.

4. Research usually divides the principal problem into more manageable sub-problems. The whole is composed of the sum of its parts. That is a universal natural law; that is also a good precept to observe in thinking about one's principal goal in research. We break down principal problems much more frequently than we realize.

Let's take an everyday problem to see how it breaks down into a number of sub-problems. Suppose you want to reduce crime through environmental design. Your principal goal is to find a good design solution that can reduce crime. You soon realize, however, that at the outset some sub-problems must be considered. Here is a structuralization of the problem and its attendant sub-problems:

Main problem: **How to prevent crime using environmental design?**

Sub problems: What is the best design solution?

What type of environment deters crime?

What principles provide the best solution?

What seems like a simple primary question can be divided into at least three other questions before the principal question can be resolved. So it is with most research problems. The researcher usually cannot deal with the principal research problem in toto. To proceed logically, one should closely inspect the principal problem because research will soon cause the appropriate and, in fact, necessary sub-problems to float to the surface. By resolving them, we finally resolve the main problem.

If researchers don't take the time or trouble to isolate the lesser problems within the major problem, their research projects become cumbersome and unwieldy. From a design standpoint, therefore, it is expedient to reduce the main problem to a series of logical sub-problems that, when resolved, will resolve the main problem.

5. Research is guided by the specific research problem, question, or hypothesis. Having stated the problem and the attendant sub-problems, each sub-problem is then viewed through a construct called a hypothesis. A hypothesis is a logical supposition, a reasonable guess, an educated conjecture. It may direct your thinking to the possible source of information that will aid in resolving the research problem through the resolution of each attendant sub-problem.

The Framework of Landscape Architecture Research

Controlled

The concept of control implies that, in searching for the cause and effect of a problem in relation to two variables, the research should minimizes the effects of other factors affecting the relationship. In landscape architecture, this can be achieved to a large extent by confining to the field of study or environment within the research framework. The impact of the variables must therefore be quantified.

Rigorous

You must be stringent in ensuring that the procedures followed to answers to questions are relevant, appropriate, and justified. However, the degree of rigour varies markedly between the physical sciences and social sciences.

Systematic

The research procedures used to undertake an investigation follow a certain logical sequence. The various steps cannot be taken in a haphazard way. Some procedures must be followed in a systematic way.

Valid and variable

This concept implies that whatever you conclude on the basis of your findings is correct and accurate and can be verified by you and others.

Empirical

Any conclusion shall be drawn from the evidence collected from real life experiences or observation during the investigation and the information collected during the course of the research process.

Critical

The research process or the process of investigation must be critically scrutinized to ensure that the research is foolproof and free from defects. The process adopted and the procedures used must be able to withstand critical scrutiny.

Types of Research

Qualitative research is a method of inquiry to gather an in-depth understanding of human behavior and the reasons that govern such behavior. Qualitative research is often used as a method of exploratory research as a basis for later quantitative research hypotheses.

Quantitative Research is the use of sampling techniques (such as surveys) whose findings may be expressed numerically, and are amenable to mathematical manipulation enabling the researcher to estimate future events or quantities. Quantitative data is collected based on random sampling and structured data collection instruments to produce results that are easy to summarize, compare, and generalize. Quantitative research is concerned with testing hypotheses derived from theory and/or being able to estimate the size of a phenomenon of interest.

CHAPTER 3
RESEARCH OBJECTIVES

The purpose of doing research is to answer questions, arising from a practical need or simple curiosity. A research question is an explicit query about a problem or issue that can be challenged, analyzed and that will yield useful new information or findings. The findings must be facts, not opinions. Therefore, research has four general goals or objectives: to describe, to predict, to determine and to explain the problem. It can be carried out anywhere, on any phenomena in nature, and by anyone. Examples are:

1. To describe the historical development of landscape architecture profession: entails an attempt to provide an accurate picture of the landscape architecture history

2. To predict the impact of urban heat island on urban trees. Once it has been observed with some regularity and credibility the next step is to anticipate what is going to happen next. Are the trees dying, not growing well, or need to be replaced with hardy species?

3. To determine the causes of fear among women walking in crime prone areas. In order to suggest

    solution to the problem one has to know the causes of the problem

4.   To explain the absence of senior citizens in urban parks: One need to understand the relationship between the events that occur. There could be several explanations that need to be clarified.

Deciding On a Research Topic

Deciding on a topic for your paper can be challenging and time-consuming, but it is an integral step in writing a good paper. After researching one topic, you may find out that you were really interested in something else. Or, you may find that your initial topic was too broad. It is important that you write a paper on a topic that interests YOU! Your topic should also be specific enough to allow a thorough description of previous findings based on reading several review of literature.

How to Find and Develop a Viable Research Topic

STEP ONE: IDENTIFY A TOPIC.

If you haven't picked a topic yet, go to Suggestions for Finding a Topic

- Discuss your topic ideas with your lecturer.
- Discuss your topic ideas by referring to library collection on the topic you are interested in.
- Look over the index and the article titles in a **specialized encyclopedia** that covers the subject area or discipline of your topic (for example, garden design, environmental psychology, GIS, Remote Sensing etc.).

State your topic idea as a question. For example, if you are interested in finding out about the function of mangrove in reducing shoreline erosion, you might pose the question, "What effect does mangrove has on the protection of coastal shoreline?"

Identify the main concepts or keywords in your question. In this case they are mangrove function, shoreline erosion, protection of shoreline.

STEP TWO: TEST YOUR TOPIC.

Test the main concepts or keywords in your topic **by looking them up** in the appropriate background sources or **by using them as search terms** in the library catalog and in periodical indexes.

- If you are finding too much information and too many sources, narrow your topic by using the and operator: mangrove and shoreline protection, for example.
- Finding too little information may indicate that you need to broaden your topic. For example, look for information on shoreline erosion, rather than shoreline. Link synonymous search terms with or: mangrove or coastal forest, shoreline erosion mitigation or sedimentation, or accretion.

You may also decide on a research topic by finding about the research problem through reading, research and analysis. You might choose a general area, for instance:

- Event leading to the development of landscape architecture in Malaysia

- a well thought landscape design eg. Bali, Japanese, or Malaysian landscape garden
- design solution for storm water management

Or you could start with a more personal approach:

- something you're interested in
- something you've always wondered about but have little knowledge of
- something that is particularly controversial or currently topical something your professor mentioned in class
- something about which you know nothing, but would like to pursue

Your subject should be an intellectually challenging question or issue rather than just being "about" a person or a work.

CHAPTER 4
TYPES OF RESEARCH

The typology of research is based on the type of information sought through research activity. The research can then be categorically based either as qualitative or quantitative research. The research classification is based on three criteria: the purpose of the study (the nature of questions asked) how the variables are measured (the method used to answer the research questions) how the information is analyzed (the degree of precision the method brings to answering question)

Qualitative Research

Qualitative research produces research findings that are not arrived at by statistical summary or analysis and lack quantification altogether.(Strauss and Corbin, 1990). The data of qualitative research are mostly obtained from interviews and observations and can be used to describe individuals, groups, and social behaviours. It is often about "naturally occurring, ordinary events in natural settings" (Miles & Huberman, 1994).Qualitative research is designed to reveal a target audience's range of behavior and the perceptions that drive it with reference to specific topics or issues. It uses in-depth studies of small groups of people to guide and support the construction of hypotheses. The results of qualitative research are descriptive rather than predictive. It is generalizing a sample to a larger group of subjects, and using numbers to prove or disprove a hypothesis. For a typical study using qualitative methods, researchers tend to draw a sample of persons at random from a broader population, if possible. The researchers are interested in generating data from a large sample of study subjects so they can generalize the conclusion to others (York, 1998).

Qualitative methods involved in-depth interviews with individuals, group discussions (from two to ten participants is typical); diary and journal exercises; and observations. Sessions may be conducted in person, by telephone, via videoconferencing and via the Internet.

Qualitative research methods were developed in the social sciences to enable researchers to study social and cultural phenomena (Myers, 1997). It is data that is usually not in the form of numbers. Qualitative research is an inductive approach, and its goal is to gain a deeper understanding of a person's or group's experience.

Qualitative research involves investigating participants' opinions, behaviors and experiences from the informants' points of view. It is contrasted with quantitative research in that it does not rely on quantitative measurement and mathematical models, but instead uses logical deductions to decipher gathered data dealing with the human element. Its downside, compared to quantitative research, is that it is more expensive, has smaller sample sizes and is hard to measure.

It is a research that focuses on how individuals and groups view and understand the world and construct meaning out of their experiences. It essentially is narrative-oriented and uses content analysis methods on selected levels of communication content. Other researchers consider it simply to be research whose goal is not to estimate statistical parameters but to generate hypotheses to be tested quantitatively.

The researcher uses inductive reasoning which is reasoning "from particular instances to general principles. One starts from observed data and develops a generalization which explains the relationship between the objects observed (Schriver, 2001)."

Qualitative research has alternative research methods and data collection methods. Examples of qualitative research methods are action research, case study, grounded theory, historical methods, and ethnography. Ethnography is the study of cultures in their natural settings (York, 1998). Grounded theory is designed to develop theory through a highly inductive but systematic process of discovery. A major focus is on the observation of similarities and differences in social behavior across social situations (York, 1998). Some examples of data collection methods are interviews, field of observations, diaries, and letters.

Scientists have some criticisms of qualitative research. Gibbs (1991) believes that "the untrained observer or the practitioner whose day to day involvement in intervention hinders objective analysis may base conclusions on vivid recollection of unrepresentative events, may misinterpret what really happened and may care so deeply about clients that judgement is clouded." He assumes that social work practitioners are unable to think like a researcher and unable to realize their own biases. He seems to conclude that a practitioner is too subjective to evaluate their interventions.

Quantitative Research

Quantitative research methods were originally developed in the natural sciences to study natural phenomena (Myers,1997). This type of research is used in many different fields, such as insurance, medicine, government, education, psychology, and law. The social work profession was built on these other disciplines, so it has historically used the quantitative approach to research. Examples of quantitative methods include survey methods, laboratory experiments, formal methods, and numerical methods. These methods are now being used in almost all social sciences.

There are three primary types of quantitative research designs, experimental, quasi-experimental, descriptive, and correlational. Experimental and quasi-experimental studies are designed to examine cause and effect. They study the effects of treatments by using tests or scales. Descriptive and correlational studies examine variables in their natural environments and do not include researcher imposed treatments (Ross, 1999). They examine the relationship between two variables using tests or scales. In quantitative research, validity and reliability can be measured numerically using such tests as inter-rater reliability and test-retest reliability.

This type of research also receives some criticism. Feminists evaluators have attacked what they call the 'myth' of value-free scientific inquiry (Janssen, 1999). All quantitative data is based on qualitative judgement . . . Numbers in and of themselves can't be interpreted without understanding the assumptions which underlie them (Trochim, 2001).

Similarities and Differences

Qualitative and quantitative research have some shared aspects. Each type of research generally follows the steps of scientific method. Those steps are 1) Choosing research topics 2) Constructing hypotheses or developing research questions 3) Selecting methods 4) Collecting data 5) Analyzing data 6) Interpreting data and drawing conclusion (Schriver, 2001). They have the same beginnings. Each begins with qualitative judgements or a hypothesis based on a value judgement. These judgements can be applied or transferred to quantitative terms with both inductive and deductive reasoning abilities. Both can be very detailed, although qualitative research has more flexibility with its amount of detail.

All research (quantitative or qualitative) is based on some underlying assumptions about what constitutes 'valid' research and which research methods are appropriate (Myers, 1997). In quantitative research, methods of observation are submitted to the tests of reliability and validity to establish the credibility of these observations (York, 1998). This can be done by inter-rater reliability, test-retest reliability, criterion validity, content validity, etc. Qualitative research checks reliability and validity in the form of prolonged treatment, triangulation, and persistent observation, as mentioned earlier.

Both methods also have ways of sampling. Random sampling is preferred in quantitative research. This allows the researcher to pick a representation of a larger group and the results can be generalized to the larger group. In qualitative research, sampling is not random. The researcher is trying to find a subject or group that are especially suited to the topic area.

Qualitative and quantitative research have more differences than similarities. The quantitative approach is objective, which means that it tries to be unbiased toward its subjects and has no interaction with a study's participants. The qualitative approach is just the opposite. The researcher or observer wants to be "in the shoes" of the participant, to understand the participant's experience. Qualitative research tries to understand the subject's viewpoint, and quantitative research counts and measures behavior with scales, tools, or interventions. As we see, their approach and methods are different. The research design of these two vary, as well. Quantitative focuses on tightly controlled variables in a structured setting to provide an explanation of laws. Its emphasis is on gathering and validating knowledge through systematic, objective observations (Schriver, 2001). On the other hand, qualitative research can have more flexible variables and is more dynamic. Qualitative researchers provide students with an in-depth description of a topic or participant. Experience cannot be quantified into fundamental elements (Schriver, 2001).

CHAPTER 5

THE STEPS IN
THE RESEARCH PROCESS

he steps in the research process is using a system in working on a research project, be it a research paper, an oral presentation, or an investigation to find a solution to a research problem. The following are the steps in the research process.

1. Finding a Research topic
2. Establish a background theory on the topic
3. The Issues/Problems
4. Identify/Define/State the problem
5. Establish achievable research objectives
6. Propose hypotheses/research questions
7. Significance of the Study
8. Describing the Study Area
9. Limitations and Delimitations
10. Definitions
11. Literature Review
12. Methodology
13. Data Analysis/Discussion
14. Conclusion
15. Recommendations

Finding a Research Topic

Find a topic that is of interest to you, or if you have been assigned a topic, select an aspect or perspective of the topic that interests you.

What is your topic? Is it relevant to the current event or issue? What more do you want to know or find out?

Where do you look for research topic?

- from your own thoughts, observation and experience
- current issues in your discipline area
- from the articles, journals, internet
- expand from other people's research
- from existing dataset and other relevant document
- from any disagreement with other people's research findings

If you are having trouble selecting a topic, you may find it useful to browse magazines, journals, newspapers, reference sources, and online databases.

Examples of research topics in landscape architecture

1. The impact of urban forestry in Malaysian cities from landscape architecture perspective.
2. The role of landscape architecture in the beautification of the Islamic Centre
3. Integrating ornamental plants into the highway landscape along the North South Highway
4. Urban Watershed Management: Incorporating Best Management Practices with Landscape Architecture Solution

5. Marketing of Medicinal Plants in using Landscape Architectural Design in urban areas
6. Ecological Planning and Design Management for Urban Riverfront Park
7. Ecological considerations in the design of Urban Lake Ecology in Shah Alam
8. Integrating drainage, ecology and recreation in a campus river: A case study at international Islamic University
9. Out of the Woods into the Urban Space. Can Medicinal Plants Survive the Cityscape.
10. Crime Prevention Through Environmental Design. An Approach in Reducing Crime in The Public Parks.
11. Women's Perception of Their fear of Crime and their safety in Urban Parks Environment
12. The Impact of Urban Forestry: Cooling Solution of Cities in the Millenium
13. Determining the Physico-Chemical Aspects of Putrajaya Wetlands for Visitors Recreational Use
14. Reading the mind of landscape architects: A case study of ILAM members
15. Factors for Success in Intensive Touristic Development on the Historic City of Malacca, Malaysia
16. The dilemma of natural areas designer: Meeting the needs of the visitors while maintaining sustainability
17. Developing a Heritage Trail for Visitors In Taiping: An Exercise in Tourist promotion
18. CPTED in Squatter Areas: A case study of Kampong Medan

19. UiTM as a centre for World Class university for People with Disabilities 2005
20. Mangrove and Tsunami: Between Myth and Reality in reducing the survival Impact
21. Applying Heritage tourism model to city of Taiping Malaysia: Lessons for citizens and stakeholders
22. Comparative Study of mangrove Forest in Iriomote Island, Japan and Kukup Island, Malaysia.
23. Sustainable Stormwater Management Design Using Best Management Practice
24. Utilizing Geographical Information System to locate Potential Urban Parks,
25. Monitoring of mangrove area using remote sensing toward shoreline protection
26. Environmental considerations in a method for highway route selection.

Starting Your Research

Don't know where to begin? Need an overview of your research topic?

Reference sources such as encyclopedias, dictionaries, handbooks, and directories are good starting points for any research project or problem. They provide background or introductory information on a topic. Bibliographies or references at the end of the chapters or articles will also lead you to other sources of information on your topic.

Finding Books

The Library may have books written on your specific topic (in which case you're in luck!). In most cases, though, you will need to locate books on the broader subject area e.g. gardens, parks, etc. and check the search by keyword or subject.

Some examples of subject headings relevant to Landscape Architecture include:

Landscape Architecture—Environmental aspects
Landscape Architecture—History
Landscape Design
Landscape Ecology
Urban Parks
Water in Landscape Architecture
Cultural Landscape
Urban Design
Regional Landscape Planning
environmental perception and behaviour
computer applications for landscape architecture

Finding Articles

Why use articles? Articles in magazines and journals generally have a more specific focus than books and are more current. Newspaper articles will provide you with the most up-to-date information on current hot topics and issues in cities and communities.

The Library subscribes to many databases which allow you to search by keyword or subject for articles in various magazines, scholarly journals, and newspapers.

The following databases are useful for finding articles in your subject area

Expanded Academic Index—indexes some popular publications and core scholarly journals in many disciplines, including the architectural design field. Some articles are available full-text online.

Academic Search Elite—indexes popular and scholarly publications in the humanities and social sciences, including some architectural journals. Some articles are available full-text online.

Art Abstracts—a good index to start searching for art, art history, architecture, landscape architecture, city and regional planning. No full-text articles are available but the Library owns a high percentage of the journals indexed in this database.

Architectural Index—A good index to search for information on architects, designers, design firms, and building types or categories. No full-text articles are available but the Library owns a high percentage of the journals indexed in this database.

Avery Architectural Index—a comprehensive architectural periodical index covering areas of architecture, interior design, landscape architecture, and urban planning. No full-text articles are available and many of the journals indexed are not available in the Library. You will need to request articles through Interlibrary Loan.

Science Direct—provides full-text access to more than 1800 titles, including Landscape and Urban Planning.

Finding Web sites

The Web can be a source of useful information and images. Subject directories and search engines can help you locate the most relevant and appropriate Web pages.

Just remember the following:

No single search engine indexes the whole web.

Become familiar with different search engines.

Each search engine behaves differently, so look at help screens to learn about search features specific to the search engine you are using.

Use a subject directory such as Yahoo to browse for Web pages on your topic.

Use a search engine such as Google to enter your search terms.

Try Alta vista to search for images.

Here are some representative examples of web sites related to Landscape Architecture:

Project for Public Spaces is a great source for information on people and projects that involve public spaces and communities.

American Landscape and Architectural Design, 1850-1920 is a great resource for images of cities, specific buildings, parks, estates and gardens, representing the work of Harvard faculty such as Frederick Law Olmsted Jr., as well as other prominent landscape architects.

The Center for Land Use Interpretation is a research organization involved in exploring, examining, and understanding land and landscape issues."

Parks, Recreation and Tourism Resources provide good research topics in human and environmental design

Research begins with a question

During the course of your occupation as landscape architect some of the following questions may come to mind:

What are needs of the senior citizens in an urban environment?

What are the best design solutions for people with disabilities?

How can we reduce crime in the park by environmental design?

What are the best horticultural practices for maintenance of street plantings?

These research questions will generate suitable landscape architecture solution

How can we design a park that reduces immoral activities?

What type of park design can reduce vandalism in the park?

Why female students in landscape architecture perform better than male students?

What are the similarities and differences between Japanese and English gardens?

Refining the research questions

1. Investigations into reducing immoral activities in the park
2. Studying the pattern of vandalism and providing effective solutions
3. Comparison factors on the performance of male and female students in the parks and amenity management.
4. Identifying the similarities and differences between English and Japanese Gardens.

The Research Question

What makes a good research question? There are certain criteria you should follow to develop your research question.

1. Be concise. As with all writing, you must state the parameters of your research question clearly so that your audience will know exactly what you are interested in finding out.

2.   Be specific. A good rule of thumb is that you should avoid broad and general questions. After deciding your topic of interest, spend some time thinking about what exactly you are concerned about researching. For example, a question that asks what is the root of society's problems will take you several, if not an infinite number of lifetimes to answer.

3.   Make sure you can answer your research question with data. In constructing your question, you should ensure that there some feasible way to gather data that will answer your question.

Writing an introduction/establishing a background theory on the topic

The purpose of an introduction in a research paper is to justify the reasons for writing about your topic to the reader, provide an overview of previous research on the topic

A theory is a tentative explanation invented to assist in understanding some small or large part of the reality around us (Tichenor, 1981). It is a set of concepts or constructs, definitions, and propositions that presents a systematic view of phenomena by specifying relations among variables, with the purpose of explaining and predicting that phenomena. A concept is a mental construct that represents some part of the world, inevitably in a simplified form. Terms like family and social class are concepts. For example, social class varies, with some people being identified as middle class and others as working class. Concepts are also terms that refer to the characteristics of events, situation, behaviours, groups and individuals that we want to study. Some typical concepts include race, vandalism, immoral activities, preferences, environmental design.

What does a theory do?

A theory or concept explains, summarizes and predicts. According to Von Wright (1971), theory serves two major objectives: To predict the occurrence of events or outcomes of experiments, and thus anticipates new facts. The other is to explain, or to intelligible facts which have already been recorded. It acts as a guide for research as well as a lead to a fruitful research area

According to Bunge (1971), a construction of a theory is to:

1. Systemize knowledge by establishing logical relations among previously disconnected information and generalizations of ideas.
2. Guide research either by (a) positioning and formulating fruitful problems or (b) research questions and by gathering of new data and selecting variables or (c) by suggesting new lines of investigation.
3. Guide or direct our research discussion and to fit our research results to a particular theoretical model, new or old.

In summary, theory makes our research easy, both before we start and after we finish our research. It also illustrates the logical steps we must follow during our research.

The Issues/Problems

Issues or problems are factors that are being argued where the existing research information is lacking or potentially flawed and a cause for public concern. It is a point of contention, dispute, or debate within the background information or theory. In landscape architecture issues and problems that arise can be traced to the following factors: planning, design, planting, changed or modified ecosystem, environment, management and maintenance aspects etc. It is these issues and problems that will provide the needs for the researcher to settle them by doing a research to come up with a solution. The issues and problmes Issues and problems have the potential to be solved within a research process have the potential to be solved by means of the research process.

Identify/Define/State the research problem

After the background theory has been established the next step would be to identify, define and state the research problem. This identification, definition and statement of the problem will set the direction of the research area and determines the research method and procedure. Whenever there is a need to know, to explain or to predict something, that will be the catalyst for the research process to proceed.

Be sure to define and state your research problem specifically enough that you can write about it. Avoid trying to investigate or write about multiple problems or about broad or overly ambitious problems. Vague problem definition leads to unsuccessful proposals and vague, unmanageable documents.

The research problem should tell everyone what you intend to research. The criteria for a good research problem or problem statement are as follows:

a) stated clearly, described accurately and precisely
b) posed in solvable terms by logically simplified or reduced to a number of manipulable variables or factors is connected logically to the environment from which is drawn and can be applied within that environment:
c). solved by acceptable methods and procedures with meaningful contribution to your area of interest.
d). t has not been solved previously.
e). sharpens the focus of the intended study.
f). the solution to the problem shall be making a potential and significant contribution to the body of knowledge.
g). explain exactly what you want to accomplish in the study.

Examples of problem statement

1. This study is to develop a model for a proper park management system using GIS method
2. The aim of this research is to determine the minimum scale of fees for public entry to the park
3. This research is to determine the design solution that lead to reduction in crime in the urban parks
4. This study is to determine the impact of the location of golf courses close to the water bodies
5. The purpose of this study is to analyze the effect of privatization of public parks on a. attendance and

participation b. the income of the agency c. the effects of the public perception of the agency

Establishing achievable research objectives

Research objectives are both problem and task oriented. They are categorized as general and specific objectives. General objectives are addressed to the problem area as a whole, whereas specific objectives are concerned with detailed problems and sub-problems. Use the following adjectives to write out your objectives:

To determine
To describe
To evaluate
To predict

Generally, the objectives are embodied in hypothesis formulation and testing, to substantiate, refine, or dispute a particular theory. The basic objectives of all types of research are of course the same, that is to explain, predict, and/or describe a social, behavioural, historical, marketing, or the phenomena of subject of interest.

Examples of objectives are:

To describe the attitudes of students toward quality of teaching

To determine the problems faced by first year students in landscape architecture program

To establish the relationship between healthy living and recreation activities.

To explain why students have positive attitude towards some lecturers and not for others.

Propose the hypotheses/research questions

Theory and research are inseparable and hypothesis is the essential link between them. A theory may be incorporated based on several substantiated hypotheses. A hypothesis on the other hand is generally derived based from a theory or theories that you have built up during the research process. It can be formulated using a formal statement or in the form of research questions.

Definition of hypothesis

A hypothesis is an educated guess about the phenomenon being studied. "Educated" meaning that is goes beyond mere speculation. That is, the hypothesis is a translation of information gathered from theories, other research, and casual observation.

It is a conjectural statement of the relation between one or more variables. It is always stated in a statement or declarative sentence form (Kerlinger, 1973). Other definitions of hypothesis are as follows:

A type of idea that states two or more variables are expected to be related to one another. a proposition that is stated in testable form and that predicts a particular relationship between two or more variables an intelligent guess involving a condition that has not yet been determined but merits exploration. a potential solution to a problem or as an explanation of some unknown fact. an element of relationship that, if found true, would be a logical inference and offer support of some explanation of the theory being studied.

In research, a hypotheses is the investigator's prediction or expectation of what the results will show. It is a conjectural statement of the researcher's expectations about how the variables in the study are related. In short, a hypothesis is a prediction that is made prior to data collection.

Why researchers use hypotheses?

Researchers use hypotheses because they serve a number of important purposes:

1. The hypothesis provides a focus that integrates information. We often have hunches about predictions, based on experience, previous research and the opinion of others. By forming a hypothesis the researcher synthesizes the information to make the most accurate prediction possible. Usually the researcher draws heavily on not logically related to the previous literature, the importance of contributions of the research is questionable. The overall credibility of the study is diminished.

2. The hypothesis is testable. It provides a statement of relationships that can be tested by gathering and analyzing data.

3. The hypothesis helps the investigator know what to do. The nature of the hypothesis directs the investigation by suggesting appropriate sampling, instrumentation, and procedures. It helps the researcher keep focused, specific scope that is not too general.

4. The hypothesis allows the investigator to confirm or disconfirm a theory. Hypotheses help advance knowledge by refuting, modifying, or supporting theories.

COMPONENTS OF A HYPOTHESIS

Often, hypotheses are expressions about how changes in one variable will result in changes in another variable. Hence, the key components of the hypothesis are the variables

Variables

Variables are any measurable conditions, events, characteristics, or behaviors that are controlled or observed in a study.

ISSUES TO CONSIDER WHEN FORMULATING A HYPOTHESIS

To be testable, a hypothesis needs to be formulated precisely and the variables need to be defined clearly.

Variables

A variable is something that varies and can be measured. It has several synonyms, such as changeable or unsteady. For example, hair color is a variable that can take on the values of red, brown, black, blond and, these days, green, orange, and even puce. Other variables would be height (expressed as short or tall), weight (128 lbs. or 150 lbs.), age at immunization (6 weeks or 18 months), time off work, age groups (teenagers, youths, adults) income groups (upperl, middle, lower) and political party affiliation. These variables can be described as dependent or independent variables.

Variables are the empirical or measurable counterpart of a construct or concept

For causal studies: independent and dependent variable

For correlational studies; predictor and criterion variables

Independent variables are varied or manipulated by the researcher in an experiment

1. Dependent variables are those variables under study and affected by the independent variables

A **dependent** variable represents the measure that reflects the outcomes of a research study. It is measured to see whether the treatment or manipulation of the independent variable had an effect. Think of a dependent variable as the outcome that may depend on the experimental treatment or on what the researcher changes or manipulates.

Independent: A variable that is manipulated to examine its impact on a dependent variable. An independent variable represents the treatments or conditions that the researcher controls to test their effects on a particular outcome. Independent variables must take on at least two levels or values. For example, if a researcher were studying the effects of gender differences (the independent variable) on language development (the dependent variable), the independent variable would have two levels, male and female.

Independent variable	Dependent variable
Smoking	Cancer
Career talk	class performance
Age	marriage
Marriage	job career
Television	violence

Entrance Fees   willingness to pay

Environmental Design   safety

Well kept garden   crime

Crowding   behaviour

Example of a hypothesis where variables are applied

Landscape architecture students in **highly** motivated peer groups will experience more **positive** response in their studio group assignment from members of their peer group (who are also highly motivated) than from non-members.`

To recap:

Causal and Correlational

Causal studies analyze "cause and effect"

Elements of cause and effect

Cause precedes effect in time

Empirical pattern between cause and effect

No 3rd variable or alternative explanation

Cause (1st variable); effect (2nd variable); something other than these would be the 3rd.

Correlational studies

These simply look at the strength and direction of the relationship between two variables

They can't account for cause and effect

E.g., higher levels of education are positively related to income

Definition of the Variables

Although there are some variables of interest that are immediately measurable/observable (e.g., height, gender—these are overt variables), most variables in psychology are not immediately measurable/observable (e.g., love—these are latent variables). Hence, to achieve a clear formulation of the hypothesis, an operational definition needs to be provided for those variables that will be studied. That is, the researcher needs to describe the actions (or operations) that will be used to measure or control the variables that will be used in the study.

Independent (antecedent) versus dependent (outcome) variables

As mentioned earlier, hypotheses are often expressed as how changes in one variable will result in changes in another variable. This is merely a simplified case in which the hypothesis contains only two variables. However, many hypotheses include more than one variable. Also, most studies often have more than one hypothesis. When multiple variables and hypotheses are involved, the study becomes more complex. Thus, it may be helpful to note which variables will be used as independent (antecedent) variables and which will be used as dependent (outcome) variables.

In the most simplest terms, the independent (antecedent) variable is the one that the researcher uses to predict changes in other variables. Hence, the "other variables" are the dependent (outcome) variables.

Sources of hypothesis

The sources for hypothesis may come from common sense, observation of the pehomena, theories, past research and practical problems

Common sense

They are things that the majority of us believe to be true. Testing a hypothesis based on common sense can be valuable because not all common sense notions turn out to be correct. Sometimes, common sense can be contradictory. We are familiar with the phrases, "boys will always be boys", "birds of a feather flock together", "absence makes the heart grow fonder", "well kept garden reduce vandalism" "shade trees reduce temperature better than palm trees". Researchers may wish to test whether either of these notions is true or under what conditions each may prove to be true.

Observation of the phenomena

Observation of events happening around us can provide questions that may merit hypothesis. When something happens for example, hillside erosion, peat fires, contaminated upstream rivers, increase rate in crime in the neighbourhood vandalism in the park, we may ask why it happened.

Theories

Theories helped to organize and explain a number of facts specific to the phenomena in order to provide a framework of understanding the events or phenomena. These theories will provide concepts around which one can organize and explain these events and phenomena. Theories can generate new knowledge or findings by noticing new aspects of phenomena. This is done by testing the hypothesis to correct the theories.

The significance of hypothesis

It is a tentative solution we are searching for during the course of our investigation

It is the central part of our investigation and provides a study with focus. It tells you what specific aspect of a research problem to investigate. Whatever is discussed in a research is generally centered on hypothesis substantiation or rejection, and whatever conclusion may be drawn is usually a summary of hypothesis formulation, testing and implications.

Functions of hypothesis

To summarize existing findings

To delimit the scope of investigation so as to concentrate on manageable problem

To provide general guides to determine variable of factors to be examined

To determine the design, procedure, and method of research

To be tested for its substantiation or rejection.

To interpret the data and findings

To reaffirm, revise, or even destroy a theory

All the hypothesis usually involved in measurement of two or more variables.

How Are Hypotheses Written?

1. Salt in soil may affect plant growth.
2. Plant growth may be affected by the color of the light.
3. Bacterial growth may be affected by temperature.
4. Ultra violet light may cause skin cancer.
5. Temperature may cause leaves to change color.

6. Trees with large canopy may reduce the temperature.
7. Parks with forest-like environment may attract wildlife.
8. People's perception of comfort living may varies with their income.
9. An exclusive neighbourhood may reduce crime.
10. More open spaces in a neigbourhood may contribute to healthy living environment.

All of these are examples of hypotheses because they use the tentative word "may." However, their form is not particularly useful. Using the word may does not suggest how you would go about proving it. If these statements had not been written carefully, they may not have even been hypotheses at all. For example, if we say "Trees will change color when it gets cold." we are making a prediction. Or if we write, "Ultraviolet light causes skin cancer." could be a conclusion. One way to prevent making such easy mistakes is to formalize the form of the hypothesis.

Example of Formalized Hypotheses: If parks with forest-like environment is related to wildlife, then parks with forest-like environment will attract wildlife to inhabit them.

If leaf color change is related to temperature, then exposing plants to low temperatures will result in changes in leaf color.

Notice that these statements contain the words, if and then. They are necessary in a formalized hypothesis. But not all if-then statements are hypotheses. For example, "If I plant more flowering plants then many butterflies will be attracted." This is a simple prediction. In a formalized hypothesis, a tentative relationship is stated. For example, if the planting of more flowering plants are related to the attractions of the butterflies then more flowering plants should be planted. "Then" is followed by a prediction of what will happen if you increase or decrease the presence of flowering plants. If you always ask yourself that if one thing is related to another, then you should be able to test it.

Formalized hypotheses contain two variables. One is "independent" and the other is "dependent." The independent variable is the one you, the "scientist" control and the dependent variable is the one that you observe and/or measure the results. In the statements above the dependent variable is flowering plant and the independent variable is butterfly.

The ultimate value of a formalized hypothesis is it forces us to think about what results we should look for in an experiment.

Past research

Past research often generates future and further research. A different research approach from the past research may be used to test the hypothesis if the previous hypothesis is disputed

Practical problems

Research based on several hypotheses may be conducted to solve problems that may require immediate solutions. The effect of the Tsunami disaster in 2004 has generated a number of researches on how to prevent the occurring of the phenomena or to reduce its impact on human and environment.

Definition or Terminology

A definition or a terminology is a concise statement explaining the meaning of a term, word or phrase. The term to be defined is known as the definiendum (Latin: that which is to be defined). The form of words which defines it is known as the definiens (Latin: that which is doing the defining).A definition may either give the meaning that a term bears in general use (a descriptive definition), or that which the speaker intends to impose upon it for the purpose of his or her explanation (a stipulative definition). Stipulative definitions differ from descriptive definitions in that they prescribe a new meaning either to a term already in use or to a new term. A descriptive definition can be shown to be right or wrong by comparison to usage, while a stipulative definition cannot. A persuasive definition named by C.L. Stevenson, is a form of stipulative definition which purports to describe the 'true' or 'commonly accepted' meaning of a term, while in reality stipulating an altered use, perhaps as an argument for some view, for example that some design elements used in a garden design is subjective. Defining the terms used in the statement of the problem or sub problems helps to clarify or reduce the possibility of these terms or words being misunderstood.

Limitations

Major limitations include time, costs, access to resources, approval by authorities, ethical concern, and expertise

Delimitations

Confined to the area of investigation

Exercise

Start doing a research on anything that is of interest to you and the scope is within the landscape architecture area. Follow the format based on the lecture note given in the lecture notes above. Begin with a research title, background theory, problem statement, research objectives, hypotheses, terminologies, limitations and delimitations. Submit at the beginning of next class session.

CHAPTER 6

WHAT SHOULD BE WRITTEN IN CHAPTER 1 OF YOUR RESEARCH?

The Chapter Outline
Introduction and background of the study
Research Questions
Research problem/Problem statement
Research aims and objectives
Significance of the study
Study area
Definition of variables/or key terms
Delimitations and limitations

Introduction and background of the study

The purpose of the introduction is to provide the reader with background information needed to understand the rest of the research. The nature of introduction is conditioned by the level of your research and the diversity of the audience and their familiarity with the research project. At Ph. D. level, the introduction should be written in more depth than at research at Masters level. As for audience level, the more diverse the audience, the more extensive is the introduction (Kinnear & Taylor, 1991). There are five components of writing a good introduction. The first one is establishing the problem leading to the study. The second component is reviewing the literature about the problem, thirdly identifying deficiencies in the literature about the problem. The fourth component is targeting the audience and noting the significance of the problem for this audience, and finally identifying the purpose of the research (Creswell, 2009).

1. Establishing the problem leading to the study (background information)

Without an introduction it is sometimes very difficult for your audience to figure out what you are trying to say. There needs to be a thread of an idea that they will follow through your paper or presentation Cooper & Schindler, 2011). The introduction gives the reader the beginning of the piece of thread so they can follow it. An introduction should provide the relevant background information for the research (Malhotra, 1993). The introduction presents the problem being investigated. It is intended to give the reader an appreciation of the broad context and significance of the type being researched (Cozby, 1981). It must clearly explain the nature of the problem being researched. Start with sentences that introduce your topic to your reader. All introductions should contain information that allows the reader to fully understand the topic, the topic's relevance, and the article's thesis before proceeding to more in-depth examination or exploration. The language should be very simple and straight to the point. Keep in mind that most of your readers will find a lot of interest in introductory materials. This is what will determine their interest into further reading.

2. Reviewing the literature

In reviewing the literature, the nature of any previous research on a similar problem should be reviewed. You do not have to give too much detailed information on reviewing the literature; save that for the body of your paper. Make this literature reviewing as interesting as you can. Through it, you can hook the readers and get them very interested in the line of thinking you are going to develop in your project. The researcher should next specify the problem to be investigated, provides the underlying rationale, and establishes why it is important. Some references to the literature should be made, although it should not be extensive to resemble a review of literature, which is more properly done in chapter two. The literature cited in the introduction, coupled with the researcher's own thoughts, should be to stimulate interest and to establish the underlying rationale for the research (Baumgartner & Hensley (2006).

3. Identifying deficiencies in the literature

Deficiencies in past literature exist because the topics may not have been explored fully or the research has not been replicated or repeated. These deficiencies should be mentioned once or twice to signify the gaps or shortcoming of the research conducted by other researchers. When identifying deficiencies in past literature the researcher might use the following tips:

a.   Cite several deficiencies in other research that will pave the way for your research to contribute to a new knowledge

b.   Identify specifically the deficiencies of other studies e.g. methodological flaws, variables overlooked, unsuitability of application etc.

c.   Write about areas overlooked by past studies including topics, significant implications, the treatments used.

d.   Discussed how your proposed study will remedy these deficiencies and provide a unique contribution to the field of knowledge.

4. Significance of the problem

In this section the researcher will convey the importance of the study, who will benefit from it and a clear rationale for embarking on the study. It is good to provide two to three reasons that this study will contribute to the scholarly research and literature in the field, improve the present management practices and application, improvement in the existing policy.

5. Identifying the purpose of the research

This section deals with the problem statement after the problem has been identified in the background information. This will help to provide a focus of the study to be conducted. This will be followed by the research objectives, hypothesis or research questions.

In summary, an introduction is a preamble or introduction about the research problem. It describes the general feeling about one specific issue under study or that has been investigated. Past research and theories relevant to the research problem are described in detail. Why it is important to highlight the issue?—To portray the importance of the phenomenon of the interest. Generally, this section requires information, statistically, statements or gaps in the previous studies or concerned by somebody (e.g. professionals, industries or government). The introduction should be a statement of concepts, facts, theories, personal concerns and actual conditions in life, which has led the researcher to believe that there is a research problem worth studying. Concept: is a term that describes an abstract idea formed by generalizing from particulars and summarizing related observations.

Identification of problem can be done by highlighting the key theories, concepts and ideas in what appear to be some of the underlying assumptions in the area of research. Why are these issues identified important? What need to be solved? There should be sufficient background material to help the reader to understand and appreciate the scope of the problem. Write a few statements that intend to provide a clear picture of the problem area, the specific question or questions that the research is designed to investigate. Within 5-7 pages the background information based on theories, facts, personal concerns, observation and actual conditions in life should give a concise picture of the area of investigation.

What is a theory?

A theory is a set of general propositions, used as principles of explanation of the apparent relationships between certain observed phenomena. It is a set of interrelated variables, definitions and propositions that presents a systematic view with the purpose to explain the natural phenomenon. Prediction and understanding are two purposes of theory. The theory should provide the background for the study. One uses theory deductively and places it toward the beginning of the plan for a study. The objective is to test or verify a theory, rather than to develop it. The theory becomes a framework for the entire study. The researcher tests a theory by using hypotheses derived from the theory. These hypotheses or questions, in turn, contain variables that are measured by using items on an instrument. Qualitative research consistent with inductive model of thinking and a theory may be emerge during the data collection and analyse phase of the research or be use relatively late in the research process as a basis for comparison with other theories.

An example of a well thought introduction:

The introduction should give a clear idea of the problem and the basic thrust of the research. The introduction typically begins with a general statement of the problem area, with a focus on a specific research problem, to be followed by the rational or justification for the proposed study. Write an opening sentence that stimulates interest as well as conveys an issue to which a broad readership can relate.

Specify the problem leading to the study. What issue establishes a strong rationale or need to conduct the study?

Indicate why the problem is important.

Consider numeric information.

Consider short sentences for impact.

A reader also needs to know what research has been written about the problem.

Discuss how the present study addresses these deficiencies.

Propose research questions to highlight the problem

Examples of sources of problem identification are:-

Own experience or the experience by others.

Through observation
Literature gaps
Theory

Problem Statement

A problem might be defined as the issue that exist in the literature, theory or practice that leads to a need for the study. This section is focusing on a problem, be sure to define and state it specifically enough that you can write about it. Avoid trying to investigate or write about multiple problems or about broad or overly ambitious problems. Vague problem definition leads to unsuccessful proposals and vague, unmanageable documents. Naming a topic is not the same as defining a problem. By asking oneself, what is the rationale for the study? The problem begins to become clear. Keep the following essential points In mind as the 'problem' is presented and composed:

Research problem must be stated clearly with one or two sentences. The point of the problem statement is to outline the problem to be addressed, variables are identified and suggest a method by which the problem could be solved. It is the broad problem that the researcher will examine more precisely in the hypotheses (Emory & Cooper 1991).

Criteria for evaluating research problems

A good research problem clearly, explicitly, and concisely communicates to the reader and user of research the specific question addressed in the study. The following criteria can be used to judge how well the problem accomplishes this purpose.

1. The problem must be researchable. A researchable problem is one that can be answered by collecting and analyzing data.

2. The problem should be important. The results of research need to have theoretical or practical importance. Problems that have already been well researched or are trivial should be avoided. Most studies that make contributions are original in purpose and/or method. Theoretical importance is determined by the contribution of the study to existing knowledge. Are the results meaningfully related to what is already known? Do the results add new knowledge or change the way we understand phenomena?

   Practical importance suggests that the results will have immediate use in day-to-day activities or decision. How will the results be used?

3. The problem should indicate the type of research. The language used in research problem should indicate whether the study provides a simple description, a relationship, or a difference. A simple description implied from such problems as these: How many landscape architecture students have skills in autocad? What factors are most important in reducing users conflict in public parks? A relationship describes something and also indicates how two or more variable may be related. It can be expressed statistically as either a correlation coefficient or in differences between categories of the independent variable.

For example, the following problems imply a relationship that probably uses some type of correlation coefficient:

What is the relationship between heritage buildings and preservation?
Is there a relationship between effort in river beautification and the perception of the public?
Is the lecturer's experience and motivation influence the students' desire to perform better in a class participation?

Other relationship problem analyze the differences between categories of the independent variable. For example:

Do urban population differ in their attitude towards natural environment and built environment?

Some research problems imply more than a simple relationship. They suggest a particular type-a casual relationship. Here the intent of the research is to test a cause-and-effect relationship between the independent and dependent variables. This category includes all the experimental research and some types of non-experimental research. Typically differences are emphasized in the problem statement, and often the word effect is used. E.g., What is the relationship between crime prevention through environmental design and gated community? Here are some difference questions that imply cause-and-effect relationships:

Will method A result in higher achievement than method B?

Is there a difference in temperature between streets ith trees compared to cities planted with palms?

What is the effect of hedges that separate pedestrians and vehicles?

Does the feelings of safety of the design students who frequents the studios at night will increase with the installation of better lighting facilities within the faculty?

4. The problem should specify the population. The population is simply the people that the researcher wants to investigate. A good research problem identifies, with a few words, the most important distinguishing characteristics of the population. Too much detail about the subjects will unnecessarily repeat the full description in the subjects section of the research report. Hence the description of the population in the research problem should be concise yet informative. Here is the problem that is too vague about the population:

Do students who practice their drawing skills improved more than who practice less?

Here is the same problem with a description that is too specific:

A good level of specificity would be this:

Do low-ability, first semester landscape archltecture students who practice their drawing skills improved more than those practice less?

5. The problem should specify the variable. A good problem statement of a relatively simple study will name the variables and how they may be related in a single sentence. Often these will be independent and dependant variable. Variable are described, like the populatlon, with a moderate level if specificity. "A study of the effect of teacher workshops on teacher morale as measured by the Smith Morale and Attitude Scale" does provide a dependent variable, but there is more detail than necessary and still the problem does not communicate much about the independent variable (workshop). Here the design of the study will contribute to the description of the independent variable. If two groups of teachers are being compared, one who attends the workshop and who does not, a better, more informative problem would be "Is there a difference in the morale of teachers attending a teacher workshop compared to teachers who do not attend? The independent variable is more than just named; it is described.

Research problems that are more complex because of having several independent and/ or dependant variables may need to be stated in more than one sentence. The first sentence typically includes either the main variable or a general term to represent several variables. It is followed by one more sentence that describes all the variables:

The purpose of this study is to investigate the attitude and perception between male and female students of landscape architecture toward their studio assignment. The investigations are based on class attendance, CGPA scores and amount of time spent on completing their assignment.

6. The problem should be clear. The importance of a clear, concise research problem cannot be overemphasized. One purpose of the research problem is to communicate the purpose of the study a result that occurs only if the reader's understanding of the purpose is consistent with the researcher's. Also, a clear research problem reflects clear thinking by the research. A clear problem includes terms that are not ambiguous. Ambiguity is seen when different people, reading the same thing, derive different meanings from what is read. If a term or phrase can mean several things, it is ambiguous. Terms such as effect, effective, achievement, aptitude, methods, curriculum, and students, by themselves, are ambiguous are vague. The terms are too general and should be replaced or modified so that the meaning is clear. A vague statement such as "what is the effect of sex education?" needs much more specificity. What is meant by "effect" and "sex education"? What grade level? What type of study is it? It is also best to avoid technical language or jargon that may not be well understood by others, unless the report

is intended to be read only by other professionals in a specific field. A successful problem indicates unambiguously the what, who, and how of the research by using declarative sentences such as "The purpose of this study is to . . ." or questions such as "What is the relationship between . . . . '; "Is there a difference between . . ."; "How do . . . ."; "What is . . ." Either type of sentence is acceptable, and you will find both in literature.

Research Objectives

Research objectives are the aims and purposes of doing the study. It is a set of objectives that will focus your research investigation. Also it helps to solve the problem i.e. to find answers to the research questions. This will act as a guide to the researcher on their research hypothesis and conceptual framework. Research objectives should be stated in the form that can answer the questions; for example:-

To identify . . .
To investigate . . .
To examine . . .
To explore . . .
To describe . . .

What is the difference between aims and objectives?

Aims are a general statement about what you wish to achieve, objectives are specific measurable targets that can be ticked off once achieved. An objective may be thought of as either a solution to the problem or a step along the way toward achieving a solution; an end state to be achieved in relation to the problem. The sentence often used improperly as a problem statement, i.e., "The objective of this project is to . . . . ," is properly completed by the inclusion of the objectives.

Research Questions

A research question is an explicit enquiry about an issue or problem that can be examined, challenged, analyzed to yield useful new information. It is the reflection or opinions of the researcher. Therefore research questions are question about the problems that the researcher would like to know more by asking questions. What are the issues the researcher likes to know/understand or highlights? A research question builds upon your initial statement about what you want to study, and explains it in such a way that variables are identified and the nature of the data that you intend to collect is clear. It should also make clear how the data will be analysed to add to the general knowledge and to solve the problem.

There are 5 types of research questions:-

What . . . (descriptive—frequency or test of differences consisting of one variable) e.g. What are the causes of immoral activity in the public parks? Here immoral activity is the variable

Why . . . (causal relationship—experimental) e.g. Why immoral activities often occurs in public parks

Where (specifics—location. environment etc.) e.g. Where do the immoral activities occur

When . . . (indicates the time, period and probability) e.g. When do the immoral activities happens?

How . . . (relationship—influence, effect, etc)

What is the difference between the research problem and research questions/hypotheses

The research problem or the problem statement usually refers to decisions; in contrast, the research questions and hypotheses usually require information for their solution. The research questions or hypotheses are the specific questions that the researcher will gather data about in order to satisfactorily solve the research problem (Emory & Cooper 1991).

Significance of the study

It describes the significance of the study for select audience. It identifies who can benefits from the study. (Example: designers, planners, park managers, researchers, visitors) What can be gained from this study? What are the new concepts, measurement, theory that the researcher used?

Study area

This section reviews the study area in general and investigates the role of case studies on the site area.

Definitions, delimitations and limitations

Definitions

Define the terms or scientific words giving the meaning of all terms used in the statement of the problem or sub problem that have any possibility of being misunderstand or that individuals outside the field of study may not understand.

The definition must not be too wide or too narrow. It must be applicable to everything to which the defined term applies (i.e. not miss anything out), and to no other objects (i.e. not include any things to which the defined term would not truly apply). The definition must not be obscure. The purpose of a definition is to explain the meaning of a term which may be obscure or difficult, by the use of terms that are commonly understood and whose meaning is clear.

Delimitations

The delimitations of a study are those characteristics that limit the scope (define the boundaries) of the inquiry as determined by the conscious exclusionary and exclusionary decisions that were made throughout the development of the proposal. Among these are the choice of objectives and questions, variables of interest, alternative theoretical perspectives that could have been adopted, etc. The first limiting step was the choice of problem itself; implicit are other, related problems that could have been chosen but were rejected or screened off from view.

Limitations

It is the constraints on general and utility of findings that are the result of the devices of design or method that establish internal and external validity. Examples are time, costs, access to resource, approval by authorities, ethical concerns and expertise. The most obvious limitation would relate to the ability to draw descriptive or inferential conclusions from sample data about a larger group or area. Outlining basic limitation is the influence which either cannot be control or the result of delimitations imposed by the researchers.

Delimitations and limitations therefore, are parameters for a research study to establish the boundaries, exceptions and reservations in both qualitative and quantitative studies.

Use delimitations to address how the study will be narrowed in scope

Provide limitations to identify potential weakness of the study e.g. of delimitation

Initially, this study will confine itself to interviewing and observing the park users' behaviour in Taman Tasik Shah Alam.

CHAPTER 7

WHAT SHOULD BE WRITTEN IN CHAPTER 2 OF YOUR RESEARCH?

Literature Review

A literature review is an examination of the research that has been conducted in a particular field of study. It surveys scholarly articles, books and other sources (e.g. dissertations, conference proceedings) relevant to a particular issue, area of research, or theory, providing a description, summary, and critical evaluation of each work. The purpose is to offer an overview of significant literature published on a topic. It is an overview of the subject, issue or theory under consideration. It may offer new interpretations, theoretical approaches, or other ideas. Knowledge is cumulative: every piece of research will contribute another piece to it.

Hart (1998) defines literature review as:

The selection of available documents (both published and unpublished) on the topic, which contain information, ideas, data and evidence. This selection is written from a particular standpoint to fulfill certain aims or express certain views on the nature of the topic and how it is to be investigated.

It is the effective evaluation of these documents in relation to the research being proposed.

Seeks to describe, summarize, evaluate, clarify and integrate information in the field of study.

Identifies the dimensions of current work in the field or provides a comprehensive and up to date review of the topic.

In the literature review the author or researcher describes the result of prior research that is considered related and relevant to the study at hand. In any research undertaking, your own research problem is always central. The literature review then acts as a form of aid and assistance in tackling your problem.

To increase the breadth of knowledge in the subject area

To assess the current state of research in the field and identify trends

To identify seminal works and authors in your area

To identify possible gaps in the literature or the research

To demonstrate your command and understanding of your field

To provide the background to and justification for the research undertaken

To give your research a conceptual framework It is the very basis of your research: the platform on which you will build your argument.

A review of related literature therefore will benefit your research in the following ways:

It can reveal investigations similar to your own

It can suggest a method or technique of dealing a problematic situation which may suggest avenues or approach similar to your problem.

It can reveal to you sources of data which you may not have known existed

It can introduce you to significant research personalities.

It can help to see your own study in historical and associational perspective.

It can provide you with new ideas and approaches which may not have occurred to you.

It can assist you in evaluating in your own research efforts by comparing them with related efforts done by others.

Help us sharpen our research focus

Help us formulate our hypothesis

Help us to redefine the problem or problem area.

Build bridges between the different areas that you review

Provide evidence that you have read a certain amount of relevant literature and that you have some awareness of the current stated of knowledge on the subject.

Activities in progress at the same time and reading may even spill over into the data-collecting stage of your study

Justify and support your arguments

What have others already learned from the current knowledge? This will allow you to make comparisons between other people research with your research.

Demonstrate your familiarity with your field of research

Impress your readers with the scope of your reading

All the literature review should be focused around your research problem. The first criterion in literature review is "exhaustiveness". Any relevant information that is available should be obtained and examined. The next criterion is selectiveness. The review will depend on how relevant and specific the selected literature to the problem.

Search for existing literature based on: searching for existing literature in your area of study reviewing the selected literature developing a theoretical framework develop a conceptual framework

Search for literature review can be conducted from the following sources:

1. Indexes (keywords)
2. Abstracts (dissertations, theses)
3. Search online
4. Periodicals
5. Journals
6. Books
7. CD-ROMs

Look for Author, Title, Subject, expert
Writing the literature review
Read other literature reviews
Create a unified theme, or a line of thought
Use a system to organize your materials

Work from an outline and combined together all the review of literature to further strengthen your research framework.

A literature review is therefore:

A select list of available resources and materials with a strong relation to the topic in question, accompanied by a description AND a critical evaluation and comparative analysis of each work.

A good literature review will help you do the following:
Narrow your research focus;

Pose questions that might not have previously occurred to you;

Build a knowledge base for future research.

What is the Purpose of a Literature Review?

To demonstrate the scholarly ability to identify relevant information and to outline existing knowledge. to identify the 'gap' in the research that the study is attempting to address, positioning the work in the context of previous research and creating a 'research space' for the work.

To evaluate and synthesise the information in line with the concepts of the research.

To produce a rationale or justification for the study.

How to begin a search for literature Review?

a. Go to the indexes (keywords) and abstracts (a summary of an article or study) e.g. dissertation abstarcts, psychological abstracts

b. Search online (internet)

For example, try doing a search for literature reviews concerning landscape and Malay gardens. Please note the search structure:

- the first word is the subject of the search, "landscape"
- we want to limit our search to "Malay gardens" in landscape.
- as a result, we have "Malay gardens and landscape"
- we also want to limit this search to literature reviews, so we type in "review"

- because we want to search for "literature reviews" and the synonym phrase "review of the literature", we will conduct the search using an adjacency operation.
- lastly, we will type in the word "literature"

Therefore, this search will be executed as: Malay gardens and landscape literature review.

Literature Review in Landscape Architecture

Despite our new-found dependence on multi-media, academic fields continue to advance through critical review and analysis of the literature. Reading materials that are published in one's academic or professional domain are essential to advancing landscape architecture research. They focus on the place of landscape architecture in the wider scheme of ideas and theories which attempt to explain, interpret and guide our understanding of the relevant literature resources. Human discourse on the past and present attempts to record impressions, needs, and/ or organizational patterns of natural and man-made landscapes assists professionals and lay people in assessing changes in the landscape. It also aids in developing heightened awareness and new levels of sensitivity toward the environment. Often times, this leads to strong partnerships in the protection and enhancement of our cultural and natural resources. Review of critical theory and meaning associated with a broad landscape architecture literature and grounding in the fundamentals of research design

Blindly accepting all this is written on a subject, however, without critically evaluating the context and/ or content can be devastating to a field. Landscape architecture is a very broad field of study. By reviewing the literature, both past and present, one can gain an appreciation of the depth and breadth of issues, affecting landscape design, planning, and management. Whether one examines landscapes through the romantic eyes of the fictional writers or the scientific eyes of the researcher, all of these works contribute to our understanding, of the landscape and its impact on humankind.

Use databases

Academic researchers find more information, more efficiently, by reaching into scholarly journal databases to build bibliographies for their papers and dissertations. Union Institute & University's Research Engine is a useful place to begin accessing academic databases for use in scholarly projects.

There are basically three types of sources that you will consult throughout your review of literature. The first are **general sources**, which provides clues to the location of references of a general nature on a topic. Such sources certainly have their limitations, but they can be a real asset because they provide a general overview of, and introduction to, a topic. They also provide clues as to where you should go for the more valuable or useful information about your topic. Examples of these resources are newspapers, news weeklies, popular periodicals and magazines etc.

The second source type is **secondary sources**. These are accounts of the actual research that has been done. Secondary sources are those that you seek out if you are looking for a scholarly summary of the research that has been done in a particular area or if you are looking for further sources of references. They appear as reviews of research or as other original works including abstracts.

The third source is the **primary sources**. These are the original reports of the original work or experience. These information can be found in journals, abstarct and scholarly books, educational resources information centers (ERIC), or documentaries.

Nowadays many of the information can be quickly obtained from several search engines. These are as follows:

Lycos, Hotbot, Metacrawler, Ilor, Google, Internet Sleuth, Dogpile, Ask Jeeves, Excite, Yahoo, AltaVista. However, precaution must be taken to check the authenticity of these information.

How should I write my Literature Review?

When writing the literature review, it is important that the literature review should has a logical and coherent structure, and that this structure is clearly apparent to the reader. It is a good idea to let the readers know exactly how the review is organised. The literature review begins with a discussion of the related literature from a broad perspective. It then deals with more and more specific or localized studies which focus increasingly on the specific question at hand.

Discussing, Evaluating and Critically examining the literature

The literature review needs to critically examine the texts that relate to your research question, rather than to just list what you have located. Therefore, you must link the literature to your research question, demonstrating how it supports or extends the topic or the existing knowledge in the area. You should also highlight the strengths, weaknesses and omissions of the literature, providing a critique of the research. Hence, the language used in a literature review is often evaluative and demonstrates your perspectives of the literature in relation to your question.

Make your 'voice' clear

Your 'voice', that is, your perspective, position or standpoint, should be clearly identifiable in the literature review, as in the thesis as a whole. However, in the literature review because you are writing about other people's work it is easy for your own 'voice' to be lost. The literature review then reads like a mixture of different tones and arguments. It is important that, firstly, your theoretical position is clearly and strongly stated and that your critical evaluations are an integral part of this. Secondly, it is important that your language indicates your own or other writers' attitudes to the question or issue.

Writing the Literature Review

Writing a literature review lets you gain and demonstrate skills in two areas: information seeking: the ability to scan the literature efficiently, using manual or computerized methods, to identify a set of useful articles and books critical appraisal: the ability to apply principles of analysis to identify unbiased and valid studies.

Define or identify the general topic, issue, or area of concern, thus providing an appropriate context for reviewing the literature.

Point out overall trends from other sources, by other writers in what has been published about the topic; or conflicts in theory, methodology, evidence, and conclusions; or gaps in research and scholarship; or a single problem or new perspective of immediate interest.

Establish the writers' reason (point of view) for reviewing the literature; explain the criteria to be used in analyzing and comparing literature and the organization of the review (sequence); and, when necessary, state why certain literature is or is not included (scope).

Writing the body of literature

In the body, you should:

Group research studies and other types of literature (reviews, theoretical articles, case studies, etc.) are according to common denominators such as qualitative versus quantitative approaches, conclusions of authors, specific purpose or objective, chronology, etc.

Summarize individual studies or articles with as much or as little detail as each merits according to its comparative importance in the literature, remembering that space (length) denotes significance.

Provide the reader with strong "umbrella" sentences at beginnings of paragraphs, "signposts" throughout, and brief "so what" summary sentences at intermediate points in the review to aid in understanding comparisons and analyses.

Writing the summary of the literature review

In the summary, you should:

Summarize major contributions of significant studies and articles to the body of knowledge under review, maintaining the focus established in the introduction.

Evaluate the current "state of the art" for the body of knowledge reviewed, pointing out major methodological flaws or gaps in research, inconsistencies in theory and findings, and areas or issues pertinent to future study.

Conclude by providing some insight into the relationship between the central topic of the literature review and a larger area of study such as a discipline, a scientific endeavor, or a profession.

CHAPTER 8

WHAT SHOULD BE WRITTEN IN CHAPTER 3 OF YOUR RESEARCH?

Methodology

C hapter 3 describes the major methodology used to collect the data which will be used to answer the hypotheses.

The methodology chapter should have separate sections to cover:

- justification for the methodology in terms of the research problem and the literature review.
- the unit of analysis and subjects or sources of data
- instruments or procedures used to collect data.
- administration of instruments or procedures
- limitations of the methodology
- evidence that the assumptions of analytical techniques were met.
- computer programs used to analyse the data, with justifications for their use.
- ethical issues.

What method will you use?

Archival Data Collection Method:

Archival data collection is a research method that involves using previously published or documented findings available in public records or cultural artifacts. Some examples of archival data include school or military records, personal journals, medical data, photographs, videotapes, pre-recorded television shows, magazines and newspapers. Using archival data allows a researcher to identify specific trends over time and to compare historical information from different time periods. This method of primary research involves "digging up" historical or rare materials that have not been widely investigated in recent years. Once you find the archival materials you want to look at, you will essentially do a content analysis in order to find an interesting issue tied to current debates to which your new research can add a significant perspective or example.

Experimental Data Collection Method:

Experimental data collection is used to detect cause-and-effect relationships. It is a type of research in which the investigator varies some factors (variables), keeps others constant, and measures the effects on randomly assigned participants. The independent variable is any variable that the researcher manipulates (the proposed cause) to see its impact on another variable. The dependent variable is any variable that is being measured (the proposed effect) and is thought to be affected by manipulation of the independent variable. The experiment is therefore a research method for investigating cause and effect under highly controlled conditions. This type of research is usually explanatory. Experiments are typically designed to test a specific hypothesis, or an unverified statement of a relationship between variables. The ideal experiment involves three steps leading to the acceptance or rejection of the hypothesis. The three steps are: (1) measurement of the dependent variable, (2) exposure of the dependent variable to the independent variable, and (3) remeasurement of the dependent variable. One strategy for controlling outside influences is to divide subjects into an experimental group and a control group. The experimental group consists of participants who receive the experimental treatment; the control group receives no treatment or some other treatment. If the two groups are alike in all respects except for the variation created by the manipulation of the independent variable, then any differences between the two groups on the dependent variable is thought to be due to the manipulation of the independent variable.

Survey/Questionnaire

The survey is a method of primary data collection based on communication with a represenative sample of individuals. It provide quantitative information about people and the social world. The census is one example of a survey in which the same questions are asked of the selected populations. Survey is well structured and piloted, it can be a relatively cheap and quick way of obtaining information. All respondents will be asked the same questions in, as far as possible, the same circumstances. This method is conducted to obtain information which can be analysed, patterns extracted and comparisons made. It asked respondents about their **attitudes, beliefs, opinions, self classification, knowledge and past and**

present behaviour. The answers are summarized in the form of tables, graphs and percentages.

a. **Attitudes/ Beliefs/ Opinion**

Do you think every neighborhood should have access to public park?

Which age groups are the most frequent visitors to the park?

What is the biggest problem facing the park users?

Do you think your park caters for all types of age groups?

b. **Characteristics**

What time do you go to the park?

How often do visit the park?

What level of education do you have?

Are you single, married, divorced?

Do you jog everyday?

When was the last time you visited Taman Negara?

Are you a member of SOLAR?

c. **Expectations.**

Do you think you are satisfied with the cleanliness of the park?

Do you plan to use the park regularly?

Do you think regular enforcement in the park save vandalism?

d. **Self-classification.**

Do you like to visit the park by yourself or with your friends?

Do you consider yourself hardworking, not working hard, or moderately hard working?

e. **Knowledge.**

Have you tried the new playground equipment?

Is steel playground equipment better than wood?

Which species of timber is the most durable in the tropical climate?

f. **Past or present behavior.**

During your school days were you Involved in the outdoor activities?

What do you do during your free time?

Advantages of survey.

- Quick
- Inexpensive
- Efficient (less manpower)
- Cover a wide geographical area.
- Accurate.

Disadvantages.

- Lack of external validity.
- What they answer is not what they would prefer to do.
- Not suited to illiterate or semi-illiterate.

Survey Terminologies.

Population.

A collection of people living in a designated geographic area.

E.g. Klang valley, UITM Shah Alam, FSPU. Adult visitors to Hutan Bandar, Johor Bharu.

Sample.

A subset or tiny section of a population. Could be one person, a group of people.

Representative sample.

A sample whose members posses characteristics in the same proportion as a whole population e.g. building supervisors in Klang Valley are representative of building supervisors in Malaysia.

A random sample: a sample drawn in population in which every member of the population had an equal chance to be picked.

Sampling ratio:

The ratio of the size of the sample to the size of the target population

E.g. 150/50,000 = 0.003%

Sampling frame:

Specific list of population that closely approximates all the elements in the population telephone directories, drivers license, student matrix numbers.

Sample size:

The larger the sample size, the more accurate is the results or generalization.

For novice researchers use as large samples as possible. Large sample maximizes the possibility that the means, percentages, and other statistics are true estimates of the population.

But large sample size ill cost you time and money.

How much then?

Varies but as the saying goes the larger the better

E.g. 113,000 out of 200 million population in the US<0/05% but represent accurate representation of people's belief and religious affiliations.

What is the exact figure for representative sample

None! The most important is the sample is representative of the population.

Steps in Survey Research

A. Design and planning Phase

I.   Decide on the type of survey (mail, telephone, interview, face to face, foucs groups), type of respondent and population.

II. Develop the survey instruments/questionnaire

- Write questions to measures variables/ hypothesis
- Decides on response categories
- Organize question sequence.
- Design questionnaires layout

III. Plan a system for recording answers

IV. Pilot tests the instruments and train interviews if necessary

V.   Draw the sample

- Define target population
- Decide on the type of sample
- Develop sampling frame

- Decide on sample size
- Select sample

B. Data Collection Phase

1. Locate and contract the respondents
2. Make introductory statements or provide instructions
3. Ask questions and record answers
4. Thank respondent and continue to the next despondence
5. End data collection and organize data

Steps in conducting survey

STEP 1: Decide what you want to accomplish (the research objective)

A clear and well defined purpose of doing a survey. Must be able to state a testable hypothesis.
Details to be thought about

1. Type and number questions
2. Variable to be assessed
3. How to generate a representative sample
4. Preparing of a questionnaire
5. Scoring and analyzing data

STEP 2: The sample

To generalize from a sample of population.
Must have a clear delimitation of subject inclusion.

Must a systematic and unbiased mean of a representative sample.

E.g. what is the criteria for an adult? Age 21 and above? How are park use and non-park users are defined?

The sample must be able to provide the researcher with the desired information.

How many subjects or respondents will be interview?

Must be a large enough sample to be a representative of a population.

STEP 3: Instrument Development

Type of questionnaire

List the variables be measured.

A variable is a concept that varies

E.g. gender is variable (female or male)

Martial status (married, single, divorced, widowed)

Type vandalism (stealing, graffiti, displacement, damage, destruction)

A person attitude (strongly against park hour opening 24 hours a day, prefers 8 hours a day)

Simple Common Sense Rules in Questionnaire Design

a. Use simple language
b. Each question should ask one thing only
c. Each question should not have escape route e.g. Don't know, no comment, it depends
d. Get the question order in the right
e. Test the questions

Types of questions to be asked

1. Structured data collection

Either open ended or close ended

Open ended: the respondent is free to express his opinions

Disadvantage:

Too subject and difficult to interpret, analyze and quantify.

Takes longer to answer and difficult and respondent.

Close ended question-More objective making them easier to analyze.

Type of close-ended questions:

➢ Ranking e.g. list the top ten recreation activities.
➢ Scaled responses-Likert scale assign values to statement indicating the degree of agreement or disagreement.

During recreation activities do you feel happy?
1.never 2.sometimes 3.all the time

1. Fixed alternative / categorical response

Yes or No

Principle of Constructing Good Questionnaire

a. Avoid jargon, slang and abbreviation
b. Avoid ambiguity, confusion and vagueness
   E.g. do you jog regularly?
c. Avoid double-barreled questions.
   E.g. do you go to the park both during the morning and evening time?

    d.   Avoid leading questions
         E.g. you don't destroy the amenities in the park do you?
    e.   Do not ask respondent's difficult questions
         E.g. how many times have you visited the park five last year?

A survey researcher uses a sample, a cross-section or a portion of group of people (e.g. 25 students) but generalizes result to a larger group (1500 students)

E.g. Park and amenity students do not prefer to have classes that begin at 8 o'clock in the morning.

Part time students prefer to start class at 7 o'clock in the morning.

Asking the questions

    I.   Be thoroughly familiar with the questionnaire

       -   Practices by reading it loud.

    II.   Ask the question exactly as they are worded

       -   Slight change in wording can distort results
       -   Ask the question in the order in which they presented in the questionnaire.

Observation

One way to collect primary data is by recording the behavioural patterns of people (subjects) as well as data on objects and events. It is a systematic and selective way of watching and listening to an interaction as it takes place. For example observing traffic flow, park users activities from early in the mornings to late evenings. It is highly suitable in park or natural setting.

Observation method is necessary when full information cannot be elicited using other methods such as survey because respondents are not cooperative or not answering truthfully.

Types of observation

Participant observation: the researcher participates in the activities of the subjects being observed with or without their knowing that they are being observed. It is a method by which researchers systematically observe people while joining in their routine activities. This method is very common among cultural anthropologists who use fieldwork to gather data for their ethnographies. Sociologists typically refer to this type of research as case studies. Such research is exploratory and descriptive. Participant observation is based heavily on subjective interpretation, and is therefore criticized by some for lacking scientific rigor.

Non-participant observation: the researcher does not get involved in the activities of the subjects or individual but remains a passive observer, watching and listening to its activities.

Problems when using observation as a method of data collection.

When subjects are aware that they are being observed, they may change their behaviour.

The possibility of observer bias. The observer record may be bias and not easy to verify.

The interpretations drawn from the observations may varies from observer to observer

There is the possibility of incomplete observation and / or recording.

Situations in which observations may be made

1. Natural: not to intervene
2. Controlled: introducing a stimulus for the subject to react to it.

The recording of observation

Narrative: records a description of the interaction in his own word. Make a brief note to be followed with a narrative. Narrative will provide a deeper insight on the observation. However, the observer may be biased in his narrative.

Mechanical: record the subjects using digital cameras, video cameras,

The primary purpose and goals of writing the methodology is to: to explain in detail the procedures for how your data were collected and analyzed allows for other researchers to critique the validity of your data and conclusions allows for other researchers to duplicate your study supports or refutes the validity of your findings

Writing the Methodology

A. Describe how the research was conducted

What method/tool/software is used
Describe the research procedure using this tool in down-to-earth, operational terms by using step by step instrumentation or by explaining using flow chart.
Describe the advantages of using this tool.
When did the research take place (month and year, duration of research)

Where did the research take place

Describe how information/data will be generated, analyzed and reported

B. Justify the procedure

-   feasible in terms of the resources and time available
-   appropriate under the circumstances for collecting the necessary type of data
-   suitable for addressing the issues, problems or question that underpin the research
-   having rigour, coherence and consistency
-   producing data that are representative, valid and reliable
-   conforming with ethical standards

C. Acknowledge any limitations to the method employed a. What unexpected factors arose during the research, and what effect did they have? b. In what ways, if any did resource constraints influence the quality of findings? c. Are there any reservations about the authenticity, accuracy, or honesty of the findings? d. Could the methods be improved further?

CHAPTER 9

WHAT SHOULD BE WRITTEN IN CHAPTER 4 OF YOUR RESEARCH?

Results and Discussions

This chapter provides the results and discussions based on the body of method used that help to describe facts, detect patterns, develop explanations, and test hypotheses.

In conclusion, Chapter 4 presents patterns of results and analyses them for their relevance to the research questions or hypotheses. Frequent summary tables and figures of results are essential, so that readers can easily see patterns in the mass of data presented in this chapter. Chapter 4 should therefore be restricted to presentation and analysis of the collected data.

Once you have collected your data, you will need to organize it and interpret it so that you can present your main findings to the reader. Your method of analysis will vary on the method of data collection, whether it is quantitative or qualitative.

For Quantitative methods, your main method of analysis will be through statistics You address the following statistics:

- Measures of central tendency (mean, mode, median)
- Measures of dispersion (range, frequency distributions, standard deviations)
- Measures of association (Chi-squared, Pearson's R, Lambda, Gamma, Somer's D, just to name a few).

For Qualitative methods, your main method of analysis may vary but a most common strategy is through coding and writing memos.

- Coding is the process of reading and labeling of field notes, transcribed interviews, documents or visual images in order to begin to compile themes.
- Writing Memos is where researchers begin to draw out initial analyses, connections, and interpretations of their codes.

Assessing your findings

After analyzing your data and determining your main findings, you should go back to the literature review and your argument/hypothesis and assess where your results fit in. By doing so, you are stating how your research contributes to our existing knowledge. Use these questions as a guide to evaluate your results.

- Do your findings suggest a new pattern that we did not about?

- Does it corroborate past research? How so?
- Does it contradict past research? How so?
- What are the implications of your results for our understanding of the social phenomena under study?
- Do your findings raise questions for future studies?

Interpreting Results

In the data analysis, the results for each question in the survey were discussed along with the appropriate statistical analysis and an illustration in the form of a table or chart. As part of the interpretation of the results, you need to go back to the findings previously discussed and interpret them in light of the sub-problems you posed as part of your research question. This sub-problem interpretation is based on the results of each research item. Whereas in the data analysis you only identify the results without editorializing or commenting on them, now we are ready to draw conclusions about the data.

As part of the interpretation, you will want to place your results in the context of your literature review. That is to say, to what extent do you have an explanation why other researchers might have reached different conclusions, or even what the implications are of your data pointing to similar results. Since your literature review drove the development of your hypotheses, it is logical that you would discuss whether hypotheses tested positive or negative as part of your interpretation.

You may present your data analysis and their interpretation together or separated into two chapters (four and five), with the first one discussing only the direct conclusions based on presentations of numbers, percentages and other hard data, and the second one interpreting the work presented in Chapter four. However, because they are so closely related, it is also a good idea to prepare and write these two chapters in parallel.

CHAPTER 10

WHAT SHOULD BE WRITTEN IN CHAPTER 5 OF YOUR RESEARCH?

Conclusions

The word "conclusions" is used or written in thesis or research reports as it complete a report and identify an outcome. The conclusion is based from the interpretation of data in chapter 4. In the conclusions section, the author comes back to the research problem or hypothesis, research objectives posed in the introduction and tells the reader what new insights were achieved.

It also describes or discuss the research findings, final decisions or determinations regarding the research problem. The conclusion of a research report is usually a very short section that introduces no new ideas. The conclusion is important because it is your last chance to convey the significance and meaning of your research to your reader by concisely summarizing your findings and generalizing their importance. It is also a place to raise questions that remain unanswered and to discuss ambiguous data. You must state your conclusions clearly.

Do not be ambiguous about them or leave doubt in your readers' minds as to what your conclusions are.

The conclusions you draw are opinions, based on the evidence presented in the body of your report that is from the data obtained. Since they but because they are opinions you should not tell the reader what to do or what action they should take. Save discussion of future action for your section on Recommendations.

Included in the conclusion are the limitations of the research to remind the reader that there are constraints or limits to the knowledge being reported.

Limitations do not mean that the results of a study are flawed or meaningless. They do, however, indicate the boundaries of or constraints to the knowledge generated by the research. One might view the research study limitations as the fence that surrounds and "limits" the new knowledge contained in the report. To decide whether to use the knowledge described in a research report and how it will be used requires you to understand the aspects of the research process, such as sampling or methods that may constrain the new knowledge.

Once you have stated your conclusions clearly, you can move on to discuss the implications of your conclusions. Be sure that you use language that distinguishes conclusions from inferences. Use phrases like "This research demonstrates . . ." to present your conclusions and phrases like "This research suggests . . ." or "This research implies . . ." to discuss implications. Make sure that readers can tell your conclusions from the implications of those conclusions, and do not claim too much for your research in discussing implications. You can use phrases such as "Under the following circumstances," "In most instances," or "In these specific cases" to warn readers that they should not generalize your conclusions.

Finally, the conclusion section of a research report usually contains recommendations for future research regarding the problem of interest. These recommendations often directly address the limitations that have been described and suggest additional studies that are needed to further build on the new knowledge generated from the study described in the report.

A jigsaw puzzle analogy is useful for understanding what chapter 5 is about. Research begins like a jumbled jigsaw puzzle about the research problem. Chapter 2's literature review starts putting the pieces together to uncover a picture, but shows that some pieces are missing and so the complete picture cannot be known. Then chapters 3 and 4 describe the hunt for the missing pieces. The chapter 5 returns to the puzzle, briefly summarizing what the picture looked like at the end of chapter 2 and then explaining how the new pieces fit in to make the whole picture clear. Findings for each research question or hypothesis re summarized from chapter 4 and explained. This chapter will be a suitable chapter to make recommendations based on the findings of the research. Implications for further research written in this chapter should help students and other researchers in selection and design of future research. Further research could refer to both topics and to methodologies or to both.

In a nutshell the final chapter of your research should contain the followings:

Summarize your main findings

Relate your findings to the conceptual ideas or past research that you discussed in the literature review

Highlight insights learned and how it contributes to our sociological knowledge

Address limitations of current research that became apparent during the progress of the research, for example, questionnaire results may indicate that age of respondents is a limitation.

Offer specific suggestions for future research

Suggest policy implications, if applicable

Suggestions

Each chapter (except the first) may have an introductory section linking the chapter to the main idea of the previous chapter and outlining the aim and the organization of the chapter. Each chapter should also have a concluding summary section that outlines major themes established in the chapter, without introducing new material.

The final paragraph of each chapter usually summarises the key achievements of the chapter. So the conclusion of chapter 1 should reach something like:

This chapter laid the foundations for the report. It introduced the research problem and research questions and hypotheses. Then the research was justified, definitions were presented, the methodology was briefly described and justified, the report was outlined, and the limitations were given. On these foundations, the report can proceed with a detailed description of the research.

CHAPTER 11

ORAL PRESENTATIONS

tudents may give oral presentations of their research either in class or at a department research symposium involving students from a number of different classes or at undergraduate research conferences. All these settings share one characteristic-the time allowed for the presentation is usually no more than 10 to 15 minutes. In this length of time it is impossible the detailed description that is included in a journal article. In general, as noted in the Publication Manual, Material delivered verbally should differ from written material in its level of detail organization, and presentation. To reach your audience the Publication Manual recommends the following:

Omit most of the details of scientific procedures, because a listener cannot follow the same level of detail as a reader can. The audience wants to know (a) what you studied and why, (b) how you went about the research (give a general orientation), (c) what you discovered, and (d) the implications of your results. A verbal presentation should create awareness about a topic and stimulate interest in it; colleagues can retrieve the details from a written paper, copies of which you may want to have available. (p.339)

A staff in the biology department of a university has developed five principles that he distributes to his cell physiology students to help them prepare the oral presentation required in his class. These five principles are listed in Table 1. Like all good maxims these five sound simple enough, but they are all too frequently ignored even by experienced researchers. The temptation described in the first principle can be best avoided by limiting your presentation to one or two main points. What are important "take home messages?" The brief time available for an oral presentation is barely sufficient to allow you to present the evidence supporting these main points. There simply will not be time to discuss any side issues.

PRINCIPLES TO FOLLOW FOR AN EFFECTIVE ORAL PRESENTATION

1. Avoid the temptation to tell everything you know in 10 minutes.
2. Cultivate a good platform presence.
3. Accompany your talk with useful visual aids.
4. Leave at 2 minutes of your allotted time for questions.
5. Practice your talk before a critical audience before you give it.

CHAPTER 12

RESEARCH REPORT AND STYLES FOR CITING AND REFERENCING

Y ou may dread the thought of plowing through some technical scientific report, especially if its loaded with statistics. But as the chapter will show, understanding such material is easier than you think. Among the secrets are knowing how research reports are structured, and not starting off with the most complicated examples. Once you get the experience reading simpler reports of social science research, you will be able to read more technical ones. From there you will acquire the expertise needed to prepare research reports of your own.

This chapter addresses two main topics; the structure of most research reports, and the styles used for referencing and citing relevant research that others have conducted.

The basic format for a research report

There is a logical structure that characterizes most scientific research reports. Familiarity with this structure not only will help you read research reports, but can also serve as a guide for writing them. The following outline depicts the components of the most scientific research reports.

Immediately following the title and author in a scientific article is a one-paragraph **abstract** (or summary). (Even though many research reports are written by more than one author, for simplicity throughout the remainder of this chapter, "author" will be used to refer to one or multiple authors.) The abstract gives readers a basic picture of the study, usually in less than 200 words. The abstract is a useful feature of scientific research reports (and other scientific articles), but it is not considered a part the *body* of a scientific report. In fact, short scientific reports (those less than a page or two in length) often have no abstract.

Introduction

The first component of the body of a research report is the introduction. It is typically divided into two subparts: the **Review of Literature** and the **Statement of the Problem** (or the **Hypothesis**).

In the literature review, the author describes the results of prior research that considered pertinent to the study at hand. The literature review section also often includes an outline of theoretical ideas that may have lead a researcher to undertake the study. (More will be said in Chapter 14 about how theory and research mutually complement one another.) In addition, the literature review often offers a practical justification for the study. A clear sign that you are reading the literature review: the author is focusing on studies conducted by others in the past rather than on any aspect of the study at hand.

The other component of the introduction-the statement of the problem-is normally only a sentence or two in length (rarely more than a paragraph). The statement of the problem tells readers precisely why this study was undertaken. Although the literature review often points out where gaps still exist in the understanding of some phenomenon, the author of a research report will end the introduction with a succinct statement of what he or she will specifically attempt to help fill. The statement of the problem serves to narrow the reader's focus onto exactly what the present study was designed to accomplish. Watch for phrases as "The purpose of this study . . ." or "This study was undertaken to . . .".

Sometimes, instead of giving a statement of the problem, the author will state a formal hypothesis. As alluded to in the earlier chapter, a hypothesis is a statement about what a researcher expects to find, rather than simply what question will be addressed. In other words, a hypothesis is more formal and definite than a statement of a problem. A researcher who is relatively uncertain as to what will be found usually offers a mere statement of the problem, but if he or she has strong beliefs about what will be found (often based on some theory), a formal hypothesis will be made.

Methods

Like the introduction, the methods section of a research report consists of two distinguishable parts. The first part is a description of the **sample** (or the subjects) included in the study. The second part offers an account of what was done to the subjects, and is called the **procedures.** Each of two subsections is described in more detail below.

In describing a sample, the author discloses who the subjects were in specific terms, so if any readers want to replicate the study, they can locate a similar group of subjects and confirm the findings. This subsection usually refers to demographic information, e.g., how many of each sex, their average age, education levels, the geographical region in which the subjects lived. Other distinctive features of the sample that would be important for researchers interested in replicating the study should also be included (e.g., how the subjects were recruited).

The procedures subsection of the methods provides an account of how the study was carried out, as well as a description of any research instruments that were used. **Research instrument** is a general term referring to a tangible object used to collect scientific data. The most common research instruments used in social sciences are questionnaires (their design will be discussed in Chapter 8). As is seen in the sample, a researcher should tell the reader enough about the procedures so that it is possible for anyone to replicate the study.

Many times, a questionnaire is so lengthy that only a sketch of it is presented. This is because journals have guidelines for limiting the length of articles. If some important features of the research instrument cannot be fully explained in a report, it is appropriate and fairly common to include a notation in the methods section that interested readers may contact the author for a copy of the questionnaire. Of course, the disadvantage of this procedure is that, as time passes, it becomes increasingly difficult to locate authors.

The methods section sometimes contain a short subsection near the end that tells the reader what statistical analyses were applied to the data and why. In other studies, however, the types of analyses are sufficiently obvious as to require no special explanation in the methods section.

Results

In the results (or findings) section, readers are told what was discovered with reference to the problem of hypothesis posed in the introduction. The results section may have several parts, all uniquely tailored to the various aspects of the study being reported. This section of a research report tends to be the most technical from a statistical standpoint. It is common to find tables or graphs in the results section.

Conclusions

In this section (also called the **Discussion** or **Discussion and Conclusions**), the author reflects on his or her findings and their overall significance. Shortcomings and pitfalls may be discussed so that future researchers can avoid them. In the conclusions section, the author comes back to the problem or hypothesis posed in the introduction and tells the reader what new insights were achieved.

The body of a scientific report is followed by a reference section and occasionally by an appendix.

Citation and referencing styles in Social Science Publications

Two of the features of the scientific method are that it is cumulative and self-correcting. These features are made possible by researchers accurately relating not only what they found but also what others have found (and who those other researchers were). Researchers are obliged to inform readers about the location of reports that they cite.

It is important at this point to distinguish between a reference and a citation. A **reference** is a listing of information about an article or a book, which can be used to locate the publication in a library (or any other place it might be stored). A **citation**, on the other hand, is a statement or notation in a body of a report, which refers a reader to a reference. In the "Suicide-Moon" report, the study by Pokorny is *cited* in the first sentence and is *referenced* at the end of the article.

Styles for citing and referencing articles vary somewhat from one scientific journal to another, but researchers are expected to follow certain rules and practices that are required by almost all scientific journals. There rules and practices are outlined below, first for referencing styles, and then for citation styles.

Referencing Styles

The following items of information are required of nearly all references to a scientific article:

Author(s)
Year of publication
Title of the article
Journal in which the article appeared
Volume (and sometimes issue)
Pages

For most scientific articles, it is not necessary to identify the issue because, unlike popular magazines (where each issue begins with page 1), in scientific journals the paging runs consecutively throughout each volume (in most journals, a new volume is begun each year).

Occasionally, popular magazine articles are referenced in scientific publications. The most common practice is to reference them just like a scientific article except that the issue would be identified (usually directly following the volume and according to the week or month the issue was released).

The required information for referencing books in scientific publications are as follows:

Author(s)
Year book was published
Title
City in which the book was published
Publisher

Many books are edited rather than authored throughout by the same person (or persons). This means that each chapter is authored by one or more separate writers. In edited books, you would reference specific chapters rather than the book as a whole. In referencing a specific chapter in an edited book, the necessary items of information are:

Author(s) of the chapters
Year book was published
Title of the chapter
Editor(s) of the book
Title of the book
Pages covered by the chapter (sometimes omitted)
City in which the book was published
Publisher

The above items for referencing articles, books, and chapters in books reflects the information that you would use to locate this material in a library or order it through interlibrary loan. These items of information are given in nearly all references, but the precise style and order in which they are presented varies from one publication to another. For example, there are variations in (a) whether the first names of the author(s) are spelled out or indicated only by their initials, (b) rules for capitalizing titles of books and articles, and (c) underlining the italicizing the titles of journals and books.

It is important that you to be familiar with at least one of the common ways that references and citations are written. As shown in Appendix B, referencing and citation styles vary from one social science journal (and book publisher) to another. Because it is far easier to illustrate referencing styles than it is to present all the rules for each style, Appendix B contains examples of the most widely used referencing styles in the social sciences. Your instructor will probably instruct you to become familiar with at least one of these styles.

Citation Styles

Within the body of a scientific report (especially the literature review section), readers will encounter citations. Citations inform readers where they can find the detailed information to support a particular argument or conclusion, because all the articles and books cited will be referenced. You should know the two main citation styles: the author-date style and the numbering style.

Author-Date Citation Style

The most common citation style currently used in the social sciences is the author-date citation style. The "Suicide-Moon" study discussed earlier provides an example of this citation style. Notice that the first passage of this article states the following:

Pokorny (1964) investigated whether a sample of contemplated suicides in Texas was clustered around the incidence of a full moon rather than a new moon. He found no association for the total sample, or for subgroups by sex and race.

To confirm this interpretation of Pokorny's study, you might want to read the article that Pokorny published in 1964. This or any other scientific article can be obtained from most college and university libraries, either in bound form, on microfiche, or through interlibrary loan.

A variation on the author-date citation style would involve rewriting the first sentence of the above passage as follows:

A study conducted in Texas found no significant association between suicide rates and incidences of the full moon (Pokorny, 1964).

Note that the only substantive difference between the two versions is that the latter from focuses attention more on the nature of the finding rather than on who conducted and reported the study. Either of these two versions of the author-date citation are acceptable.

Some articles have numerous authors, and it would be cumbersome to include them all in a citation. When citing studies with multiple authors, there are slight rule variations from one journal (or book publisher) to another. With two authors, both authors are indicated, and they are usually separated with an ampersand [e.g., (Smith & Jones, 1988)], although some journals use and [e.g., (Smith and Jones, 1988)]. Of course, if the authors are referred to in the body of the sentence, you would always use *and* instead of the ampersand [e.g., Smith and Jones (1988) contended . . .].

RESEARCH PAPER ABSTRACTS

The Strength, Weakness, Opportunity and Threat (SWOT) Analysis of Mangrove Forests in the Coastal Areas of the Tropics and Sub-tropics

Nik Ismail Azlan, Dept of Landscape Architecture,
UiTM Shah Alam, Malaysia

Abstract

Mangrove is unique inter-tidal wetland ecosystem found in sheltered tropical and subtropical shores and riverine areas. It is characterized by high temperature, fluctuating salinity, alternating oxygen and low oxygen conditions, periodically wet and dry, unstable and shifting substratum. The characteristics of mangrove forest varied regionally and locally among fringe, riverine, and basin zones. Nevertheless these mangrove forest ecosystem play an important role in providing sources of tropical fish products and bore the brunt of coastal erosion and sedimentation. This paper will discuss the S.W.O.T. analysis of the mangrove forests to provide information for the significant contribution it brings to 50% of the population along the coastal areas of the tropics and sub tropics. Hopefully there is considerable scope to improve public understanding and appreciation of the value of mangrove resources and of the benefits to be obtained from their existence.

Keywords: Mangrove, tropics and sub-tropics, s.w.o.t. analysis, eco-tourism

Introduction

Mangroves may not be found or able to survive in temperate countries such as the Netherlands, the Scandinavian and other European countries but their importance and contributions to human population within the coastal waters of the tropics and subtropics have been immensely valuable. The tsunami of 2004 in the coastal areas of Asia has emphasized the need to view the mangroves in terms of natural protection, physical barrier, economic benefits and alternative tourism activities.

The origins of the mangroves

The mangrove vegetation of the world can be divided into two broad groups.The first is mangroves occurring in the Indo-Pacific region extending from the east coast of Africa, India, Indonesia Malaysia to Samoa in the South Pacific.

Figure 1. Mangrove distribution in the world

The second group, occurs along the west coast of Africa between Mauritania and Angola, in the Americas on the east coast between Barbados and Brazil and on the west coast between Mexico and northern Peru. Indonesia has the largest total area of mangrove forest while the Sundarbans swamp region in Bangladesh and India is the largest single chunk of mangrove forest in the world. The mangrove ecosystem in Malaysia is more diverse than in tropical Australia, the Red Sea, tropical Africa and the Americas. Diversity of mangrove plant species tends to increase with precipitation, and decreases with increasing latitude.

The Characteristics of the Mangroves

Mangrove trees grow where no tree has grown before. They are able to survive inundation by salt water twice a day, and in "soil" which is unstable and poor in oxygen.

They also have to deal with swollen rivers carrying silt during the wet season, as well as violent storms that hit the coasts. To deal with salt, all mangrove trees exclude some salt at the root level, and all can tolerate more salt in their tissues than "normal" plants, often in quantities that would kill other plants. But some have more effective ultrafiltration at the root level to exclude more salt. Any salt that gets through are believed to be stored in old leaves which are later shed. These include Bruguiera, Sonneratia and Rhizophora. A few can tolerate high levels of salt in their tissues and their sap can be up to one-tenth as salty as sea water. They then secrete the excess salt through special cells on their leaves.

Although mangrove trees are adapted to grow in salt water, they require regular flushing with freshwater. They will die if immersed in saltwater all the time.

Many mangrove trees have special adaptations to give their offspring the best chance in their harsh habitat. Many provide their seedlings with a good store of food and floatation devices. In some, the fruit does not fall away when it ripens. Instead, the seed within the fruit starts to germinate while it is still on the mother tree, and the mother tree channels nutrients to the growing seedling (vivipary).

In some plants, the growing seed does not break through the fruit wall while the seed is on the mother plant but only after the fruit falls off (cryptovivipary). This is the case with Avicennia and the seed coat of its fruits drops away more quickly in water of the right warmth and salinity, usually in a spot best suited for an Avicennia seedling.

Mangroves also help in soil stabilization and erosion protection. The stability mangroves provide is essential for preventing shoreline erosion. By acting as buffers catching materials washed downstream, they help stabilize land elevation by sediment accretion, thereby balancing sediment loss. In regions where these coastal fringe forests have been cleared, tremendous problems of erosion and siltation have arisen.

The World Conservation Union's report on the global status of mangroves (IUCN, 1983) lists 61 species. Major mangrove species belong to less than 15 families but the most frequently occurring mangroves belong to the Rhizophoraceae, Sonneratiaceae and Avicenniaceae.

The most important specie is Rhizophora, with arch-formed supporting roots.

Arch forming roots of Rhizophora specie

Avicennia or Sonneratia, which both have breathing roots propping them up from the mud. Mangroves occur in areas where strong wave actions are absent. The most extensive growth of mangroves can be seen in estuaries of rivers and protected lagoons and coastal lakes. Mangroves occur in areas of high humidity and their luxuriant growth is often associated with a high rainfall. Minimum air temperature and seasonal variations in temperature are important in the growth of mangroves. As cited by Chapman (1975; 1977), the best mangrove growth and development occurs where the seasonal temperature variation does not exceed 10°C and where the air temperature in the coldest month is higher then 10°C.

Mangrove ecosystems thrives in riverine (river dominated areas), fringe (tide dominated areas) and basin (intermediate interior areas) mangroves. Fringe mangroves receive the brunt of tidal actions, and basin mangroves have the greatest diversity in tree species. The mangrove vegetation is characterized by low tree diversity, almost exclusively mangroves, with a low broken canopy. Mangrove plants have a number of highly specialised adaptations to regular tidal inundation by saline waters. These include

(i)   breathing roots which allow them to survive in anaerobic sediments,

(ii) supporting structures such as buttresses and above-ground roots which enable them to grow in unstable substrate,

(iii) low water holding potentials and high intracellular salt concentrations to maintain favourable water relations in saline environments,

(iv) foliage salt-excretion to remove excess salt from the sap.

(v)   xerophytic (water-conserving) leaves to cope with periods of high salinity stress, and

(vi) buoyant viviparous propagules for dispersal and establishment in new areas.

The benefits of Mangrove

The coastline where mangrove thrives is protected because the roots of mangroves act to trap sediments that would otherwise be washed back out by the waves.

Moreover, mangroves provide a habitat for many different species of animals, including bats, lobsters, manatees, and birds. 75% of all tropical commercial fish species pass part of their lives in the mangroves, where they encounter nursery grounds, shelter and food. Other ecosystem services provided by mangroves include protection from strong winds and waves. Mangroves' protective buffer zone helps shield coastlines from storm damage and wave action, minimizing damage to property and losses of life from hurricanes and storms.

The strangest creature living in the swamps are little fish called mudskippers. During low tide, these fish walk around the mud looking for prey. Some species have suckers on their undersides that help them to climb rocks and mangrove trees. Their prey consists of small crabs, mollusks, worms, and insects. The mangrove swamps are also nurseries for many coral fish. The swamps provide a protective area for the coral fish to develop to the point where they can travel further out into the ocean to the coral reefs.

There are many species of birds that live in the mangrove areas. This is an ideal area for these birds to live in due to the easy access to both food and resting area. Many birds have developed special characteristics to their beaks and feet to help them adapt to this environment living off of certain prey. Pelicans and other seabirds live in the canopies of the mangrove swamps. During the breeding season, they form large nesting assemblages of adult birds and their offspring called large rookeries. "Other animals that find shelter in the branches and are adapted to mangroves include bats, Proboscis Monkeys, snakes, otters, the Fishing Cat. As many as 200,000 fruit bats may roost in a mangrove. Some small fruit bats roost in mangroves on offshore islands where it's safe from predators and commute daily to the mainland to feed. The bats also contribute to the mangrove: Short-nosed Fruit Bat (*Cynopterus sphinx*) is believed to be the only pollinator of key mangrove trees (*Sonneratia*).

The roots and branches of mangroves provide an ideal site for animals to feed, mate, and give birth. A symbiotic relationship exists between many animals and the mangrove; for example, crabs feeds on the mangrove leaves, as well as other nutrients and then recycle minerals into the mangrove forest. In addition to controlling coastal erosion the mangroves can expand into the sea, a process known as accretion; this results in an increase in area of mangroves—a sort of natural land reclamation. To understand better the impact of mangroves to the coastal ecosystem it is best to describe them in terms of S.W.O.T. analysis. The analysis is to provide information for the significant contribution it brings to 50% of the population along the coastal areas of the tropics and sub tropics.

The strength of the Mangroves

Mangroves protect the coast from erosion, surge storms especially during hurricanes, and tsunamis. Their massive root system is efficient at dissipating wave energy. Likewise, they slow down tidal water enough that its sediment is deposited as the tide comes in and is not re-suspended when the tide leaves, except for fine particles. As a result, mangroves build their own environment. Despite their benefits, the protective value of mangroves is sometimes overstated. Wave energy is typically low in areas where mangroves grow, so their effect on erosion can only be measured in the long-term.

Their capacity to limit high-energy wave erosion is limited to events like storm surges and tsunamis. Erosion often still occurs on the outer sides of bends in river channels that wind through mangroves, just as new stands of mangroves are appearing on the inner sides where sediment is accreting. The amount of protection afforded by mangroves depends upon the width of the forest. A very narrow fringe of mangroves offers limited protection, while a wide fringe can considerably reduce wave and flood damage to landward areas by enabling overflowing water to be absorbed into the expanse of forest. Mangroves help to filter water and maintain water quality and clarity.

Red mangroves (family Rhizoporaceae), which can live in the most inundated areas, prop themselves up above the water level with stilt roots and can then take in air through pores in their bark or lenticels. Black mangroves live on higher ground and make many pneumatophores (specialised root-like structures which stick up out of the soil like straws for breathing) which are covered in lenticels. These "breathing tubes" typically reach heights of up to thirty centimeters, and in some species, over three meters. There are four types of pneumatophore—stilt or prop type, snorkel or peg type, knee type, and ribbon or plank type. Knee and ribbon types may be combined with buttress roots at the base of the tree. The roots also contain wide aerenchyma to facilitate oxygen transport within the plant.

The weakness of the mangrove

Despite their benefits, the protective value of mangroves is sometimes overstated. Mangrove cannot largely withstand large erosion process on its own. Mangrove trees are constantly being uprooted significantly in areas where large number of ocean going ships passed through along the Straits of Malacca, Malaysia where 90,000 ships passed through annually, hence exposing the shoreline.

Wave energy is typically low in areas where mangroves grow, so their effect on erosion can only be measured in the long-term. Their capacity to limit high-energy wave erosion is limited. Erosion often still occurs on the outer sides of bends in river channels that wind through mangroves, just as new stands of mangroves are appearing on the inner sides where sediment Is accreting.

The opportunities in mangrove ecosystem

In a mangrove swamp, one cannot simply walk about without getting soiled and dirty, unless special boardwalks have been built, and even then, the walk has to follow a set trail. There is no scenic beauty there unless one is a mangrove specialist or a forester or a botanist trying to identify tree and plant species; the tide has to be right before a boat ride can be arranged. Yes, one can listen to sounds of birds and insects, but it is difficult to actually see large birds that are often pictured in the brochures. These birds must be very shy of people or easily frightened. Eco-tourism activities within the mangrove ecosystem are one of the opportunities that should be considered. It would be possible and enjoyable to construct limited infrastructure facilities such as: boardwalks, automatic listening devices, an interpretative center, jetty, clearing the streams of broken branches, building landing places along the boating route, etc.

Touring activities such as bringing tourists to the various spots of interest, providing trained guides and giving a running commentary as they pass interesting spots along the guided tour would be examples of selected eco-tourism. Walking through the boardwalk during high tide, visitors can see small fishes darting from the jagged, twisted roots of one mangrove tree to another. The tangle of roots serves as a hiding place for young fish from larger predators. Tree climbing crabs and sea snails also avoid predators by climbing the aerial roots of mangroves. Mangrove forests provide not only refuge and nursery grounds but also food to young marine species. The fallen leaves and branches nurture the marine environment. Accommodation near the site and collecting entrance fees can be built into the cost of the tour package. Presentable eateries and souvenir shops outside the mangrove areas, serving locally available food and crafts, preferably from the brackish water where the mangrove thrives can provide added income to the local community. The opportunities presented above should benefit three main entities—the environment, local community and the visitors' enjoyment of the mangroves.

The threats to mangrove

Unfortunately, mangrove forests are some of the most threatened ecosystems on the planet because of their proximity to the ocean (prime resort/development property) and the tendency to see them as useless swamps full of all sorts of threatening creatures. Over the past twenty years, great swaths of mangrove forest throughout Southeast Asia have been cleared to create commercial shrimp and prawn hatcheries.

Ironically this form of aquaculture has come at the expense of the natural fish and shrimp hatchery. Changing coastal landscapes such as coastal development, aquaculture production and mangrove felling will contribute to the loss of ecological integrity and environmental sustainability. Once mangrove forests are damaged, recovery can be very slow. Despite replanting programs over 50% of the World's mangroves have been lost.

It is often stated that mangroves provide significant value in the coastal zone as a buffer against erosion, storm surge and tsunamis. While there is some attentuation of wave heights and energy as seawater passes through mangrove stands, it must be recognised that these trees typically inhabit areas of coastline where low wave energies are the norm. Therefore their capacity to ameliorate high energy events like storm surge and tsunamis is limited. Their long term impact on rates of erosion is also likely to be limited. Many river channels that wind through mangrove areas are actively eroding stands of mangroves on the outer sides of all the river bends, just as new stands of mangroves are appearing on the inner sides of these same bends where sediment is accreting.

They also provide habitats for wildlife, including several commercially important species of fish and crustacea and in at least some cases export of carbon fixed in mangroves is important in coastal foodwebs.

Conclusion

Mangroves are an integral part of the coastal ecosystem within the tropics and the sub-tropics. Mangroves provide habitat for many marine and terrestrial animals, birds, and insects. They also provide shoreline stabilization with their extensive root structure and build islands through a process of sedimentation. Dense mangrove stands protect shorelines from storms and surges damage and increase coastal stability. In addition to onshore provisions, mangroves also protect oceanic ecosystems. By trapping sediment, mangroves allow seagrass beds to flourish. They also filter water washed over the land that could carry harmful sediment and debris that could threaten fragile coral reefs. Mangroves therefore are necessary elements of the coastal ecosystem. They provide several ecological, socio-economical, and physical functions that are essential in maintaining biodiversity and protecting human populations along the coastal areas. The role of mangroves is very important, both economically and ecologically—as a natural resource and as protection to the environment—and both aspects cannot be separated without causing damage to the area. Mangrove tree formations contribute to the marine food web through their production of detritus, and several commercially important species of marine animals are known to spend at least part of their life cycle here. For this reason, mangroves should not only be considered as forests, but also as producers of food in the form of crabs, fish and shrimp.

Their complex architecture, combined with their location on the edge of land and sea, makes mangrove forests strategic greenbelts that have a doubly protective function. They protect seaward habitats against influences from land, and they protect the landward coastal zone against influences from the ocean. The Asian tsunami that occurred on December 26, 2004, revealed the valuable buffering functions of mangroves. After the tsunami, there is considerable scope to improve public understanding and appreciation of the value of mangrove resources and of the benefits to be obtained from their sustainable management. The explanation of sustainable management systems needs to be undertaken within the formal educational systems, but must also be offered to the general public and to particular sectors within the population such as decision makers and local people. There is a need to improve the communication and flow of knowledge between scientists, managers, holders of traditional knowledge and the wider public.

REFERENCES

Brown, S. & A. E. Lugo, 1994. Rehabilitation of Tropical Lands: a key to sustaining development. Restoration Ecol. 2: 97-111.

Chen, R. & R. R. Twilley, 1998. A gap dynamic model of mangrove forest development along gradients of soil salinity and nutrient resources. J. Ecol. 86: 37-51.

Crewz, D. W., and R. R. Lewis. 1991. Evaluation of historical attempts to establish emergent vegetation in marine wetlands in Florida. Florida Sea Grant Technical Paper No.60. Florida Sea Grant College, Gainesville. 79 pp + append. (html) http://nsgl.gso.uri.edu/flsgp/flsgpt91001/flsgpt91001index.html

Erftemeijer, P. L. A., and R. R. Lewis III. 2000. Planting mangroves on intertidal mudflats: habitat restoration or habitat conversion? Pages 156-165 in Proceedings of the ECOTONE VIII Seminar "Enhancing Coastal Ecosystems Restoration for the 21st Century, Ranong, Thailand, 23-28 May 1999. Royal Forest Department of Thailand, Bangkok, Thailand.

Field, C. D. (ed.), 1996. Restoration of Mangrove Ecosystems. International Society for Mangrove Ecosystems, Okinawa, Japan: 250 pp.

Lewis, R. R. 1981. Economics and feasibility of mangrove restoration. Pp. 88-94 in Proceedings of the Coastal Ecosystems Workshop, U.S. Fish and Wildlife Service. FWS/OBS-80/59.

Lewis, R. R. 1982. Mangrove Forests. Ch. 8, pp. 153-172 in R. R Lewis (ed.), Creation and Restoration of Coastal Plant Communities. CRC Press, Boca Raton, Florida. 219pp. (pdf, 21p, 1.4MB) http://www.mangroverestoration. com/Lewis_1982_Mangroves_CRC.pdf

Nik Ismail Azlan 2007, Mangrove against Tsunami: Between Myth and Reality, Unpublished Paper, Wetlands Conference, Thailand

Nik Ismail Azlan 2008, Demographic Profile of Mangrove Eco-tourism Visitors to Kukup Island, Unpublished Paper, Wetlands Thailand.

Stevenson, N. J., R. R. Lewis and P. R. Burbridge. 1999. Disused shrimp ponds and mangrove rehabilitation. Pages 277-297 in "An International Perspective on Wetland Rehabilitation", W. J. Streever (Ed.). Kluwer Academic Publishers, The Netherlands. 338 pp. (pdf, 21p, 1.85MB) www.mangroverestoration.com/Stevenson_et_al_1999_ Disused_Shrimp_Ponds.pdf

Turner, R. E., and R. R. Lewis. 1997. Hydrologic restoration of coastal wetlands. Wetlands Ecol. Manage. 4(2):65-72. (pdf, 8p, 2.1MB) http://www.mangroverestoration.com/ hydrologic_restoraton_of_coasta_wetlands.pdf

Tomlinson, 1995. The Botany of Mangroves. Cambridge University Press; New Ed edition (March 31, 1995)

Comparing the Eco-Tourism Potential of Mangrove Forests Between Iriomote Jima, Japan and Pulau Kukup, Malaysia based on SWOT Analysis.

[1] Nik Ismail Azlan, [2] Lili Tokiman,

Introduction

"Mangrove ecotourism" is not a new "branch" of ecotourism; it merely indicates the nature of the site visited by the tourists. Eco-tourism activities within the mangrove ecosystem are one of the opportunities that should be considered in providing economic, educational and conservation benefits. What do ecotourists expect from a visit to mangrove sites? What is the satisfaction or "utility" to be derived by tourists and visitors to see these swamps? Can it be valued? Is there a characteristic that makes ecotourism services different?Touring activities such as bringing tourists to the various spots of interest among mangrove plantations, providing trained guides and giving a running commentary as they pass interesting spots along the mangrove ecosystem would be examples of selected mangrove eco-tourism. It must be realized that the attraction of mangroves is due more to the attractiveness of the ecosystem in general rather than interest in any particular species. Iriomote Jima (Figure 1) and Pulau Kukup (Figure 2) are two islands located far apart but having common sakishimasuo (mangrove) ecosystem.

Apart from that both islands contained a number of diverse ecosystems, including a rich marine biodiversity, nature and cultural experience. Iriomote-Jima is part of the Iriomote National Park or protected state land, whereas the whole of Pulau Kukup is gazetted as Johor National

Park and a designated Ramsar site, a recognition that are deemed to have international importance and are included in the List of Wetlands of International Importance. These two islands are unquestionably a few remaining great wildernesses areas of Japan and Malaysia. Mangroves play an important ecological role and provide a valuable range of living resources in coastal areas and played a vital role in protection of coastal areas against extreme climate events. Mangroves have the ability to grow in salt or brackish water and are a life support for various types of fish, mollusks (seashells), and crustaceans (crabs, prawns and shrimps).

At the same time the mangroves in Kukup Island and Iriomote Jima are under a high level of stress due to a variety of human-induced factors including fish farming, urban development and tourism. To conserve these vital ecosystems, prompt action for the improved preservation, rehabilitation and management of mangroves is urgently required.

The issues

The authorities in both islands are committed in their efforts to protect the mangrove environment, they are concerned over the deteriorating aquatic survival and uncontrolled tourism, new development proposal, and threat to wildlife. Pollution around the mangrove forest and global warming and climate change has altered the ability of the mangrove to survive and has affected the fishing industry. Both islands are facing threats from proposed new development such as new regional growth center near Kukup Island and the establishment of hotels and resorts in Iriomote Jima. These has lead to increased concern over the possibility of threatening or endangering the mangrove ecosystem if no research efforts are done to provide suggestions and solutions to the growing problems that will pose threats to the environment in both places. On the positive side both islands provide growing opportunities for various stakeholders to benefits from

The significance of the study

Despite the problems and issues facing these two natural areas it is worth researching the possibilities of benefits that these two places can offer to the various stakeholders. This paper entails several outcome that minimizes negative impacts to the environment and to local people and at the same time provide educational, economics and conservation benefits. It will help to increases the awareness and understanding of an area's natural and cultural systems and the subsequent involvement of visitors In issues affecting those systems. It will contribute to the conservation and management of legally protected and other natural areas. Another significance of this study involve the economic benefits that tend to maximizes the early and long-term participation of local people in the decision-making process that determines the kind and amount of tourism within these two areas. The economic benefits will help to complement rather than overwhelm or replace the opportunities for local people and nature tourism employees to visit natural areas and learn more about the wonders that other visitors come to see. The two islands were selected because of the unique opportunities, similarities and differences in their resources. Both islands have quite a range of ecotourism products that can enrich one another through the sharing of the information to position them to determine the ecotourism potential to benefit the various stakeholders.

Study sites

Iriomote Island is the second largest island in all of Okinawa. It is located in 30km west of the Ishigaki Island. It is a big island to the next main island in Okinawa prefecture. It can be reached by ferry from Ishigaki. Over 90% of the island is made up of tropical and amazon-looking virgin forest. The island is part of Iriomote National Park and is perfect for hiking and canoeing enthusiasts. The island has jungles, waterfalls, as well as a number of extremely rare animals and plants. The population of the island is 2,251. The island area is 289.2 km square. Iriomote is home to resorts, campgrounds, and many small family owned inns. Most inns and resorts offer a pick up service from the ferry port. Until the end of World War 2 Iriomote was largely uninhabited due to its infestation by malaria. It was used primarily as agricultural land to grow rice. Additionally, during the war some residents of Ishigaki were forcibly made to take refuge in Iriomote, some of whom contracted malaria. After the war, the Us Forces in Japan eradicated malaria from the island, and the island has been malaria free since. Apart from tourism, the island economy is sustained by agricultural production, primarily of pineapple, and fishing. Iriomote is famous for its pineapple. It received attention in recent years as the place of dispatch of the eco-tourism, which utilized the rich natural resource.

Pulau Kukup is a mangrove island located at about 1 km offshore from the mainland town of Kukup Laut, at the South-western region of the state of Johor, and towards North-west of Tanjung Piai, Peninsular Malaysia. It is a small mangrove island (approximately 647.2 ha) surrounded by mudflats (about 800 ha). The mudflats extend up to a few kilometres on the West and Northwest of the island. The mangrove island was found to be abundant with fair amount of regenerating young growing mangrove saplings. A total of 30 mangrove tree species and mangrove associcated species were recorded. The mudflats are rich in benthic organisms. A total of 12 species of vertebrate fauna and 23 species of birds were recorded both in the mangroves and mudflats, with a globally threatened stork, Lesser Adjutant being of primary concern. Pulau Kukup was officially gazetted as a State Park under the jurisdiction of the Johor State Park Corporation (Perbadanan Taman Negara, Negeri Johor) on 27 March 1997, to promote preservation of this habitat as well as promoting eco-tourism sector and providing research avenues. There is currently no human habitation or man made structures on Pulau Kukup. However, the adjacent mainland town of Kukup Laut has distinct land use activities. Kukup Laut is a fishing village which has its seafood restaurants, chalets and floating cages.

Method

A comparative study was conducted at both islands based on the strength, weakness, opportunity and threat (SWOT) analysis and market positioning techniques (Tables 1-4). In this simple analysis, two sources were drawn from several site visits to Kukup Island between 2007-2008 and various literature reviews from the internet and articles on Iriomote Island.

Table 1. Strength Analysis Of Pulau Kukup and Iriomote Jima

Pulau Kukup	Iriomote Jima
Easily accessible by boats to the island from the	Easily accessible by boats from Ishigaki Island

fishing village of Kukup Registered as RAMSAR Site for protection and conservation purpose Untouched nature and 60 species of mangrove and associated species Controlled numbers of tourist to the island providing a suitable model for ecotourism site Accommodation available at Kukup town in the form of chalets, resorts and motels Interpretive center at the main office for educational purpose	2. Called the Galapagos of the Orient to preserve the flora and fauna with marine activities and forest trekking. 3. Untouched nature with 5 species of mangrove and Iriomote wildcat (Yamaneko-mountain cat) 4. Tourist presence are regulated through ferry services 5. There is a wide range of minshukus (Japanese hotels) offering accommodation with meals 6. Iriomote Wildlife Conservation Centre for educational purposes

Table 2. Weakness Analysis Of Pulau Kukup and Iriomote Jima

Pulau Kukup	Iriomote Jima
1. No direct enforcement or patrol against intruders who may seek mangrove and non mangrove products 2. Lack of local handicraft to complement economic activities and ecotourism activities	1. No tight control or restriction on the number of visitors to the island 2. Possibility of exploitation of mangrove products that will affect mangrove ecosystem

3. Lack of formal coordination between park administrators and tourist guides to the island resulting in low level of knowledge based or educational based visitation	3. No proper or formal guide by the park authorities for the visitors to explore the educational aspect of the mangrove ecosystem

Table 3. Opportunity Analysis Of Pulau Kukup and Iriomote Jima

Pulau Kukup	Iriomote Jima
1. Better marketing and promotion will help to position the attractions that the island has to offer	1. Local and regional marketing will spur market growth for visitation
2. Global and local economic growth will increase ecotourism	2. Japan has a large population and a higher cost of living to support increase visitation to the island
3. Has diversity of plant and animal species (including several species of migratory birds) for observation, research and education, especially for students of ecology, forestry, fishery, botany or zoology.	3. A University of Ryukyu research station established here will attract research opportunities from local and international researchers and scientists
4. The accretion process where mangroves can expand into the sea, as a result of sediment accumulation would help to increase the acreage of mangrove species	4. Increasing the acreage of mangrove in this island will further boost mangrove biodiversity

Table 3. Threat Analysis Of Pulau Kukup and Iriomote Jima

Pulau Kukup	Iriomote Jima
1. Local participation in ecotourism opportunities need to be increased 2. Wave onslaught from 100,00 ships per annum passing through the Straits of Malacca have destroyed mangrove ecosystem and eroded the island rich biodiversity 3. Oil spill from ships passing through the Straits of Malacca may cause environmental destruction to the rich biodiversity of mangrove ecosystem 4. Increasing threat from pollution may affect the visual quality of the park and decrease in the availability of nesting and feeding of local water and migratory birds 5.Erosion and sedimentation may cause a disturbance to the ecosystem 6. The majority of the tourist business are not conducted by local people	1. Encroachment by outsiders in developing tourist support is depriving active local involvement 2. Threat of extinction of 100 numbers of Yamaneko cat due to conflict between preservation and development encroachment 3. Large amount of floating garbage from the nearby sea may suffocate and destroy the biodiversity of the mangrove ecosystem 4. Garbage drift from oceanic current of Kuroshio have been a threat to wildlife and sea creatures and the trash doesn't just vanish from mangrove forests. 5. The possibility of rise in sea level due to global warming may affect the acreage of the mangrove trees. 6. Lack of full community involvement

Discussions

From the SWOT analysis the two islands share several similarities and differences that can be shared and implemented as part of the enhancement programmes to facilitate a better management and attraction package for the visitors. Both islands have strengths that can be further developed to attract a reasonable number of visitors to see involve in the educational and recreational attractions and facilities that they will appreciate.

Iriomote Island, dubbed as "Galapagos of the East" has a unique nature landscape: subtropical jungle and mangrove swamps—not seen in other part of Japan. Iriomote is an island of untouched natural beauty that can be seen by trekking along mangrove boardwalk, swimming, biking, kayaking, driving, and hiking. There are other unique ecotourism opportunities including looking for Iriomote cat or Yamaneko, bird watching, firefly watching, stargazing, and camping experience. The Yamaneko numbering about 100 is an endangered species of wild cat that are only found in Iriomote Jima. This cat is facing the threat from development and inhabit the mangrove forest. Although in 1977 the Iriomote cat was declared a National Japanese Treasure, pressures of development pose a very serious threat. One third of the island has been declared a reserve where the trapping of the cat for any reason is strictly prohibited. However, the species continues to decline. Izawa (1990) reported that the density of the cats was relatively low inside the National Park because they prefer forest edges, coastal areas and lowlands, most of which are outside the protected areas. Part of their habitat has now been declared a wildlife protection area, and Japan's Environment Agency has set up a feeding and monitoring program, with a view to increasing their numbers. The Iroimote Wildlife Centre is staffed by researchers and students from the universities, who use radio telemetry to track the cats. Iriomote cats are endangered primarily because they are restricted to a single population. Iriomote island is promoted as a tourist location, with the cats being a major source of appeal. They have been fully protected since 1967, but new endangered species legislation does not cover habitat protection, and the government is now investigating ways to expand protected area coverageYamaneko therefore is the added attraction to this island.

Pulau Kukup is gazetted as the State of Johor's National Park in 1997 and a gazetted Ramsar site in 2003. Pulau Kukup is a popular tourism site. Every year there is a high flow of tourists from neighbouring countries like Singapore and Indonesia visiting Kukup town for its famous seafood. Several agencies in both islands can work in partnership to put up a proper eco-tourism activities and attractions to bring income to the Johor National Park and local communities. This is to promote ecotourism activities that will not harm the mangrove forests and sustain the local environment. In June 2003, Johor State Park Corporation developed some facilities at Kukup island to promote the ecotourism industry. A boardwalk and a suspension bridge overhanging the mangrove vegetation have been built for tourists to appreciate nature more closely. A tourist information cum education center has been established at Kukup Laut Town. Biological diversity in Kukup island is high. There are 30 species of true mangrove Leptotilus javanicus (Lesser Adjutant Stork). Wetlands International in collaboration with

Johor State Park Corporation (PTNJ) and funding from Keidanren Nature Conservation Foundation started a one-year conservation project on Pulau Kukup mangrove island. The project was carried out from June 2004 till May 2005.

The objectives of the project include:

- To promote the importance and significant values of Kukup mangrove
- To promote the implementation of an environmental education and awareness programme among the local community and visitors to Kukup wetland

Both islands offer the opportunities to be developed as ecotourism and research sites for both tourists and scientists alike. Pulau Kukup's potential tourists are from Malaysia, Indonesia and Singapore while Iriomote Jima has Japan to tap the tourists. However, several limitations in the number of tourists and provision of facilities should be planned to maintain sustainability of the tourism products.

The government can play a role in making ecotourism in both islands more enjoyable by putting in place the infrastructure: adding a few more boardwalks for viewing to preserve mangrove vegetation from being trampled, automatic listening devices, an interpretative center, jetty, clearing the streams of broken branches, building landing places along the boating route, etc. The private sector will arrange the tours and bring the tourists to the various spots of interest. The locals will provide trained guides, local activities, homestay programmes and sell local products to the tourists. Tourism in harmony with the environment and local community will in turn guarantee the sustainable development of the mangrove environment and local communities. For these two islands the challenges will be in terms of environmentally-friendly tourism to position ecotourism firmly in the strategy for biological diversity to benefit both nature and human.

Undoubtedly a few of the visitors to these two places are people who are seeking recreation value rather than the education value. It can be achieved through organizing more tourism and recreational activities based on the natural recreation and bird migrations. The existing natural recreation could be expanded to include special events, festivals and activities such as mangrove treasure hunt, family outings and company sponsored natural activities. Others to be included are special marine tours, bird tours, bird watching events and bird watching facilities provided at appropriate times of the year. Information on the links could be provided in a tour guide information pack. The weakness of the education program in these places is lack of skill and knowledgeable workers about the biological aspect, interpretation and language barrier such as English, Japanese, Korean and other languages. Update brochures in several languages should therefore serve as information booklet. Apart from that there should be an increase on the information technology of the park by keeping up to date information on the areas' biodiversity and research findings. Staff training must be continuously conducted to ensure expertise in both recreational and educational abilities to cater for the needs of the tourists.

Some of the threats facing the Pulau Kukup National Park are pouching, tree cuttings, and macro benthic harvesting and near shore fish harvesting. A few cases of tree cutting have been reported yearly. Most of the people that are caught by the enforcement unit are the local community itself. A more realistic approach will be needed to deal with these issues. The approaches might include education programs, the development of alternative livelihood options and more efficient passage through the legal process for those apprehended.

Infrastructure development is an important supporting factor for the future growth of the destination. Fabricius (2001) indicated that the physical image and infrastructure of the destination are key determinant of the quality of visitor's experience. Murphy et al (2000) found that the level or lack of infrastructure affect tourist experience and that tourism infrastructure is an important predictor of both destination quality and perceive trip value.

The technology system of both areas are still low and can be upgraded. Some of the technology that could be transfer is the management information systems computerized reservation system and information technology.

In terms of economic impact the involvement of local community is important. They should be leading in guiding and arranging activities for the visitors with cooperation with the Pulau Kukup Park Authority or Iriomote Jima National Park Administrators.

Staying in a homestay, the tourists will be made to feel like part of the family due to the warmth and hospitality of the villagers. This will bring income to the local community and help them realized the importance of the mangrove areas as an economic contributor to their family. "Multiplier effects" are often cited to capture secondary effects of tourism spending and show the wide range of sectors in a community that may benefit from tourism. This has a lot of potential for both places. A good example is the economic revenue for the local community is by involving in homestay programmes coordinated by the park authorities or with joint cooperation among the villagers themselves. Tourists visiting the mangrove forest will be exposed to another aspect of interesting living experience with the locals. Being welcomed into a villager's house is a truly intimate experience and allows the visitors to take a privileged look into the real lives of the local community. Staying and eating with a family gives the tourist the chance to exchange and interact with the community on a mutual level. Therefore, community support is important for tourism, as it is a factor that affects the community and also contributes to their economic well being. Communities therefore need to understand the relative importance of tourism to their region, including tourism's contribution to economic activity in the area.

The threats or dangers to these two special areas are factors that should be seriously taken into consideration. In Pulau Kukup oil spill from ships along the Straits of Malacca and the felling of mangroves due to soil erosion must be constantly mitigated. Compensation from the ship owners and mangrove protection are some the measures to be taken to maintain a healthy mangrove environment. Pulau Kukup has suffered from unplanned development and reclamation of the Kukup waterfront villages by fishermen. The villages with about 200 illegal houses built on reclaimed mangrove swamp land are not within the local district council's jurisdiction. Thus, it is without a proper waste disposal system and residents dump their garbage into the sea, causing serious pollution. Another source of pollution is the 70 fish farms cradled in the sheltered waters between the Kukup shoreline and Pulau Kukup. The island is also hit by ships dumping sludge and numerous oil slicks.

In the case of Iriomote Jima garbage disposal and waste products circulating from the Kuroshio current will affect the mangrove environment and if not disposed off regularly may affect tourist activities. Trash drifting across the Pacific from neighboring countries is posing problems for Iriomote Island in the Yaeyama region of southern Okinawa Prefecture. A study conducted by Professor Hareyuki Yamaguchi of the National Defense Academy of Japan says garbage, trash and junk from homes, as well as discarded fishing equipment, has found its way to Iriomote Jima. Yamaguchi identified more than 7,000 pieces of garbage, including plastic bottles and containers, plastic fishing buoys, and fishing nets drifting in the waters. More than 90% of the garbage drifts in from other countries, including about half from China, and 20% each from Taiwan and South Korea. He says oceanic currents such as the Kuroshio current, most likely brought the trash. Mangrove roots are essential filters to the Iriomote Island, stopping soil erosion. Island habitat includes shrimps, crabs and wildcats. Yamiguchi says his concern to wildlife and sea creatures is that "trash doesn't just vanish from mangrove forests. Before rotting garbage causes damage to the island by emitting toxic substances, the government, in cooperation with neighboring countries, must implement measures immediately to prevent pollution in the area".

Market Positioning

The driving force behind any attraction is consumer demand. In the case of ecotourism, the consumers are the mangrove or eco-tourists. They normally constitute a small group within the tourist population; in marketing they form a niche. It is they who will determine whether or not to visit a certain site for their outdoor recreation. As an ecotourism site, a mangrove wetland has to compete with many more appealing sites, such as a sandy beach, a marine park that allows snorkeling or scuba diving, state woodland parks, jungle trails, waterfalls, bird watching at bird sanctuaries, inland wetlands, etc. Therefore, product market positioning has to be strategized to provide an attraction that will be attract a segment of the tourists to the two islands. Product positioning has come to mean the process by which marketers try to create an image or identity in the minds of their target market for its attraction. It is the 'relative competitive comparison' their product occupies in a given market as perceived by the target market. A product's position in this case the mangrove ecosystem is how the ecotourists see the mangrove ecosystem of Pulau Kukup and Iriomote Jima. Any product attraction is valued by the perception it carries in the prospect or customer's mind. Each product has thus to be 'Positioned' in a particular class or segment. In this case, Pulau Kukup can be positioned as a nature based educational activities, and Iriomote Island as a nature based recreational activities. The position of the nature attraction has to be carefully maintained and improved. Positioning is a perception that happens in the minds of the customers or visitors. It is the aggregate perception these two islands has a particular product or attraction in relation to their perceptions of other places offering the same attractions. Iriomote Jima has almost no competition because it is the only island in Japan that offer mangrove ecosystem as a product. In fact, Iriomote Jima is considered as an island that could well qualify as Japan's last frontier. The island other attractions are beaches, rivers and waterfalls, and the rarely seen Iriomote Yamaneko.

At the same time opportunities may be opened to them by indulging in acts that give them added satisfaction—swimming, diving, snorkeling, bird watching, gazing at beautiful and unique scenery, fishing, trekking, etc. Pulau Kukup has other mangrove ecotourism competition from Larut Matang, Tanjung Piai, Kuala Gula, Kuala Selangor etc. However, Pulau Kukup can greatly benefit from the popular attraction of seafood restaurants across from Kukup Town. In fact it is the seafood attraction that has the spillover effect of these patrons to visit Pulau Kukup and be introduced to the educational activities of the mangrove ecosystem. Nearby Kg Serkat homestay programme could be extended to Pulau Kukup as part of the environmental experience for the tourists. This will help to foster appreciation and concern for the local environment and on a broader scale the mangrove ecosystem.

On the supply side, the authorities will have to scrutinize any proposed project so that it does not damage the mangrove area. There is thus a "balancing act" that has to be done by the government as a custodian of the natural heritage on behalf of future generations. In this "act" the interests of the private sector, the environment and the local community will have to be safeguarded in the name of "sustainability." In this case both islands can positively influence the perceptions through enlightened strategic actions.

Strategic actions

The two areas should be encouraged to be self-financing. One of the ways is by promoting ecotourism activities as part of the management tool for generating income from the entrance fees, activities fees and corporate donation. Entrance fee and users' fee can be charged directly to visitors to experience the mangrove ecosystems. The users fees can be charged for specific activities like scenic boat trip, camping and educational walks. Interpretation education and public awareness program for local community, visitors is the other strategic actions. This program can be in the form of written articles published to create awareness among the stakeholders. By increasing awareness of local ecosystem functions and importance, the stakeholders will develop a sense of ownership and pride in the mangrove ecosystem. Interactive curriculum for primary, secondary and tertiary school levels to educate them on the mangrove ecosystems and the importance of their conservation should be part of the programme.

The other strategic action is based on periodic assessment of the attractions to be offered in these two study sites. They are as follows:

1. Natural resources (mangrove, migratory birds, yamaneko, fauna other flora,)
2. Facilities (hiking trails, visitor centre, sheds, cafeteria, tracks, signage,)
3. Interpretation (visitor centre, information materials such as brochures, magazines, self guided interpretative trails, experienced local guides to lead interpretative hikes for organized or individual tours);
4. Educational materials in the form of simple guidebook about the mangrove ecosystem
5. Local participation (to serve as guides, park workers and labourers; provide catering services and garbage collection, homestay and other accomodations).

6. Facilities should be non-intrusive, have low impact waste disposal, be of low density but of high quality, eco-friendly, provide energy and be self-contained.

People spend money in buying goods or services because they derive satisfaction from such purchases. The same is true for travels and recreation. The tourists have spent a considerable sum of money to make the travel to a site; he or she of their entire party must pay for transportation, accommodation, food, and entrance fee. In return for these expenditures they expect to enjoy (or gain utility from) the visit, by indulging in acts that give them satisfaction—bird watching, gazing at beautiful and unique scenery, fishing, trekking, etc.

Ecotourism interests can also convince local people that their resources are as, if not more, valuable when intact than when extracted from the ecosystem. In Pulau Kukup bird watching and fish cage culture would be an added value to mangrove tourism. As for Iriomote Jima the uniqueness of Yamaneko and pineapple cultivation in this subtropical farm would provide impetus to the tourist to come to the island. Ecotourism hopes to change the unequal relationships of conventional tourism. Thus it encourages the use of indigenous guides and local products. It claims to combine environmental education with minimal travel comforts, help protect local flora and fauna and provide local people with economic incentives to safeguard their environment. When a user fee or visitor admission fee structure is imposed, real economic incentives for protected areas can catalyse their formulation (Agardy 1993).

Acknowledging that these two mangrove ecosystem can only achieve their ecotourism objectives within a context of proper management strategies, market positioning, visitors support and local acceptability, a new paradigm shift based on the above suggestions should be considered. The key message is that in order to be effective, the management of these ecosystems should take heed of the need to offer suitably educational and recreational experience and at the same time not to be above the limits of acceptable change (LAC). All human activities in natural areas cause some impact. This can be positive or negative and can vary in scale. Regular monitoring of the needs of the visitors and suitable facilities ensures that management prescriptions are successful in maintaining impacts below the LAC.

Conclusion

The SWOT analysis in this paper provides a basic research exposure and indicator on some of the issues and opportunities facing the two islands. It would be beneficial if the authoorities of both places could examine this analysis and propose a management strategy to further improve the eco-tourism potential. Both places could gain a better insight from the study of the strengths, weaknesses, opportunities and threats that prevail. The bottom line would be improving the needs and providing new opportunities for exotourists. What do ecotourists expect from a visit to these two places? The answer will depend on their interest and educational background. First-timers to a mangrove would be expecting to see an environment different fro previous experience as the mangroves are the unique forest between the land and the sea. or they want to know what a mangrove tree looks like from near. They want to know what a mangrove tree looks like from near. Others will be looking for some of the big birds (migratory or otherwise) or the Yamaneko cat that the brochures claim the mangrove to have. Some visitors would just love to enjoy "trekking" on the boardwalks while listening to the songs of birds, which are often too small to be seen without a pair of binoculars! Others look forward to the boat ride in the estuaries and waterways between the little islands. Very few would want to wade in the mud of the mangroves; hence random walks are Just not part of the enjoyment in mangroves, or other ecotours. The private sector will arrange the tours and bring the tourists to the various spots of interest, provide trained guides and gives a running commentary as the boat passes an interesting spot. Nature based tour operators must possess strong knowledge of, and an even stronger affinity for, natural areas of these two places. The knowledge must extend to the natural history of the areas' mangrove ecosystem, biodiversity, uniqueness of the flora and fauna, and an understanding of the ecological processes that sustain their existence. Operators must not only have a dedicated love and knowledge of the areas visited but also posses the skills necessary to cope with the rigors of managing a tour. These guides have to have extra-good sense of humor to make the visit interesting. With all these in place, the tourist is likely to feel he or she is getting value for money. Further research should focus on assessing the management of the parks of both places to benefit the ecotourists, mangrove ecosystem and the local community.

References

Agardy, M.T. (1993). Accommodating ecotourism in multiple use planning of coastal and marine protected areas. *Ocean and Coastal Management*, 20 (3): 219-239.

Jamal, T., & Getz, D. (1995). Collaboration theory and community tourism planning. Annals of Tourism Research, 22 (1), 186-204.

Kathryn R. (2004). Homestay: Opening a World of Opportunity. Australian International Education Conference.

Malaysia.wetlands.org/WHATWEDO/Wetlandsand WaterManagement/**PulauKukup**/tabid/1078/Default. aspx

Murphy, P.E. and Pritchard, M. 1997. Destination price value destinations: An examination of origin and seasonal influence. Journal of travel Research 35(3), 16-22

Nik Ismail Azlan, (2007) Perceiving the Demographic Profile and the Perception of the Chinese and Malays Visitors to Pulau Kukup National Park, Unpublished Paper.

Nik Ismail Azlan, Lili Tokiman (2007), Management Strategy for Natural Areas: A Case Study of Kukup Johor National Park. Proceedings of International Seminar on Wetlands and Sustainability, Johor Bharu.

Yamaguchi, Hareyuki, 14th October 2004. Garbage threatens island ecology-Japan Update.com Okinawa News.

Real Estate Property Improvement based on Hedonic Pricing Method: A Market Survey of House Buyers Preference

Nik Ismail Azlan

Dept. of Landscape Architecture

Faculty of Architecture Planning and Surveying

UiTM Sahah Alam

Abstract

Natural areas located in and near residential areas are closely related to the amenity and health of residents. Urban green spaces, water bodies and good environments provide amenities and services that contribute fundamentally to the quality of urban life. House buyers therefore increasingly expect high-quality green space and environment within and around residential precincts. Apartment with green space or water view are considered more appealing, prestigious and signify an elevated social status. Several studies were on how house buyers select their units based on urban environmental elements. The pricing methods took into consideration green view, water vicinity. The findings conclude that both green space view and the proximity to water bodies have notably enhanced residential housing price. Nearness to a wooded area which cannot be used by residents has not contributed to residential price. However, the green-space usability could be more attractive and functional. The determination of sale prices of individual units could be more accurate and desire to have view or access to green spaces and other environmental amenities. The lessons learnt from this study shows that buyers prefer green view and proximity to water bodies can help to influence buyers decision.

Keywords: Property values, Hedonic Pricing Method, Environmental values, Pricing

Introduction

Real estate market development in Malaysia is consistent with the general trend of urbanization and development. Besides location and transportation, home buyers increasingly expect high-quality green space and environment within and around residential precincts. To meet the evolving consumer preference, the design of residential grounds has become a key concern. Well-appointed outdoor spaces have been earnestly marketed to attract buyers. Apartments with green space or water views are considered more appealing, prestigious and signify an elevated social status, hence they could command a higher premium. For instance, housing property located in natural areas and away from the bustling city are earnestly demanded. Green spaces can reduce noise pollution and the visual intrusion from traffic. The risk of flooding is lower where there is plenty of urban vegetation to intercept and absorb storm water. Urban green spaces also provide a diverse habitat for mainly common bird and animal species.

In densely inhabited and urbanized areas, the provision of a pleasant view and accessibility to natural landscapes in the environs of a property, bringing passive enjoyment and relief from the otherwise congested, harsh and monotonous cityscape, is a major concern in making home buying decisions.

The amenity value provided by urban green spaces, water bodies and good environmental quality is difficult to assess and incorporate into urban planning and development. Developers have seldom objectively factored these attributes into property pricing and associated decisions. The complex factors leading to this preference and the underlying amenity value provided by natural landscape are difficult to be assessed by conventional market approaches. However, the amenity value of natural elements are usually ignored when urban landuse zoning plans are designated and when developers bid for lands for housing projects. Natural elements failed to be factored into pertinent decisions related to real estate investments. The city's valuable natural remnants could be gradually degraded or lost as a result of this general attitude. Despite the importance of such landscape features to both developers and home-makers, these environmental factors do not receive sufficient weight in current house price assessment. The main bottleneck is the lack of a scientific basis to value the worth of these landscape elements. This knowledge gap has reduced the accuracy of property value assessment (Chen et al., 2002) and hindered continued rationalization of the market.

Our urban planning policy often neglects the socioeconomic value of environmental—ecological features. Valuating such benefits could enhance understanding of their contribution to housing price and general environmental welfare. The results could help developers to rationalize their investments and decision makers to realize environmental improvement goals. A reliable estimate of the amenity value provided by various natural landscapes is important to developers interested in making good use of the potential of lands with specific natural attributes for property development. There has been no research on the possible links between landscape amenity and housing price.

The differentials between the amenity values provided by various natural landscape elements remain largely an uncharted territory. It models individual willingness to pay to consume a particular goods (usually housing) as a function of the levels of the goods' characteristics. Each property may be assumed to constitutes a distinct combination of attributes which determine the price which a potential buyer or tenant is willing to pay. This study aimed to clarify how and to what extent structural characteristics, urban green spaces, water bodies and environmental amenities affect residential housing price through the hedonic pricing method in several cities in Europe, the US and China. The findings could throw light on the effect of environmental and landscape qualities on house selection and purchase behavior in the context of our Malaysian society.

Two categories of attributes are considered, namely structural characteristics (such as housing unit size and number of rooms), and locational characteristics (such as local amenity and environmental quality).

The study objectives are as follows:

To understand whether house buyers pay a premium on environmental attributes of houses they purchased.

To verify the expected effect of variables that are supposed to affect the housing price.

To investigate which variables (environmental attributes) are considered as the most appreciated.

Related Literature

There is some evidence that the views from the windows influence the purchasing power of the buyers. Green spaces such as parks and gardens in housing areas do actually promote social cohesion amongst and between different groups in housing areas. Where most residents are living in high-rise and high-density flats commonly detached from nature, natural amenities could be perceived in a different way in comparison with cities with generous natural endowments. It could inform the decisions of policy makers and property developers concerning land selling and buying, land conversion, property development, urban nature conservation, and design of ecological green-space networks. Tyrväinen and Miettinen (2000) found that in the housing market of Salo in Finland, buyers have to pay 4.9% more to obtain a dwelling with a forest view. In Boston, it was found that when the distance to the nearest park doubles, the property price was expected to decrease by 6% (Tajima, 2003). In Emmen in the Netherlands, the price of a house with a garden bordering on water is on average 28% (7% contributed by the vicinity of a lake, 10% by a water view, and 11% by a garden) higher than the price of house without such attributes (Luttik, 2000). The different accorded values in these studies might reflect the differential provision and perception of environmental elements.

A 1973 study in Columbus, Ohio found that over 7% of a house's selling price was related to its proximity to a park and the river. A 1974 Philadelphia study significantly and positively correlated property values to the proximity of Pennypack Park. The park accounted for 33% of land value at 30 meters, 9% at 300 meters, and 4.2% at 800 meters. Property values climb because residents, especially the middle classes, se their wealth to move near an attractively designed piece of urban nature. They seek out and compete for access to community green areas, in the process driving up market prices. Studies in 1979 and 1988 found that trees contribute from 4% to 15% of a house's sale price and that a 6% tree cover distributed evenly across a developing landscape raised the value of the property by 30% over similar but treeless land. Urban green spaces, water bodies and good environments provide amenities and services that contribute fundamentally to the quality of urban life ([Shafer et al., 2000]. Due to their non-commodity and unpriced nature, and largely intangible benefits, their contribution is usually difficult to assess and quantify. Their importance to the well-being of cities and citizens is often neglected in mainstream urban planning and policy making related to development ([More et al., 1988].

Materials and Methods

To make informed policies and decisions about the effect of green space and environmental values to housing property, assessment of their benefits and values is essential ([Tyrväinen, 1997], [Luttik, 2000], [Tajima, 2003], [McConnell and Walls, 2005] and [Jim and Chen, 2006]). Various approaches have been proposed and tested, amongst which the hedonic pricing method has been widely applied in many countries to estimate the value of nature associated with settlements. The Hedonic Price Method (HPM) is a revealed preference method of valuation. The hedonic price method of environmental valuation uses surrogate markets for placing a value on environmental quality. The real estate market is the most commonly used surrogate in hedonic pricing of environmental values because the word "hedonic" comes from a Greek origin, which means, "pleasure". Hence, the hedonic pricing method relies on information provided by households when they make their location decisions. People derive pleasure by living in nice places. As the demand for land and housing increases, the price of housing increases (e.g., the cost of living in nice places is relatively high). The method can also be used in to estimate the premium placed in nice 'jobs'. The higher housing prices reveal how much people are willing to pay for the amenities in nice places. Air, water, and noise pollution have a direct impact on property values. By comparing properties with otherwise similar characteristics or by examining the price of a property over time as environmental conditions change and correcting for all non-environmental factors, information in the housing market can be used to estimate people's willingness to pay for environmental quality.

The HPM is used to estimate economic values for ecosystem or environmental services that directly affect market prices. It is most commonly applied to variations in housing prices that reflect the value of local environmental attributes. It can be used to estimate economic benefits or costs associated with: environmental amenities, such as aesthetic views or proximity to recreational sites. The basic premise of the hedonic pricing method is that the price of a marketed good is related to its characteristics, or the services it provides. The hedonic pricing method is most often used to value environmental amenities that affect the price of residential properties. The hedonic pricing method was selected in this case because: Housing prices in the area appear to be related to proximity to open space and data on real estate transactions and open space parcels are readily available, thus making this the least expensive and least complicated approach.

The model use ordinary least squares regression analysis to estimate the hedonic pricing model to relate home sale price to the parcel, structural, neighborhood, and environmental characteristics of each property. This model is written as $P = f(s1. s2. s3. \ldots si; n1, n2. n3 \ldots nj; e1,$

e2, e3 . . . ej) where s1, s2, s3 are the structural variables of the house; n1, n2, n3 are the neighbourhood variables and e1, e2, e3 are environmental variables.

It is important to note that although the hedonic pricing method may be used to estimate some of the value associated with environmental amenities, it typically does not provide a full estimate of value. The value estimated using the hedonic model reflects only the value of environmental amenities that accrue to the owners of single-family homes. Such benefits are typically highly localized. For example, in the case of open space, benefits valued by homeowners include access to recreational space and increased scenery and wildlife viewing opportunities (Thorsnes, 2002). As such, the hedonic pricing method can be used to provide a partial, not total, estimate of the value of many environmental amenities. The method's main strength is that it can be used to estimate values based on actual choices. The method is versatile, and can be adapted to consider several possible interactions between market goods and environmental quality.

The method assumes that people have the opportunity to select the combination of features they prefer, given their income. However, the housing market may be affected by outside influences, like taxes, interest rates, or other factors. The hedonic price model applied in this paper uses data on housing prices along with observable characteristics of the house and the environment to estimate the marginal implicit price of each characteristic. Hedonic pricing method is believed to be the most convincing approach in these types of valuations mainly because the technique is based on actual transaction behaviors in the market ([Hoevenagel, 1994], [Ready et al., 1997], [Hidano,

2002] and [Tajima, 2003]). It is considered relatively less controversial and less subject to interference by extraneous influences.

Data Analysis

A study was conducted by Jim and Chen (2007) exploring the impact of environmental elements with a bearing on residential housing value in Guangzhou, China, including window orientation, green-space view, floor height, proximity to wooded areas and water bodies, and exposure to traffic noise. Four large private housing estates composed of multi-storied blocks with similar design and price bracket, catering to the mass property market, were sampled. Transaction price data and structural attributes of 652 dwelling units were acquired directly from developers. Data on environmental attributes were collected in the field. Two functional hedonic pricing method models, linear and semi-log, were constructed. The semi-log model offered comparatively stronger explanatory power and more reliable estimation. High floor on the multi-storey tenement blocks contributed implicitly 9.2% to the selling price. View of green spaces and proximity to water bodies raised housing price, contributing notably at 7.1% and 13.2%, respectively. Windows with a southern orientation with or without complementary eastern or northern views added 1% to the price.

Proximity to nearby wooded area without public access was not significant, expressing the pragmatic mindset in the hedonic behavior. Exposure to traffic noise did not influence willingness-to-pay, implying tolerance of the chronic environmental nuisance in the compact city. The study demonstrates that hedonic pricing method could be applied in the Chinese context with an increasingly expanding and privatized property market. It could inform the decisions of policy makers and property developers concerning land selling and buying, land conversion, property development, urban nature conservation, and design of ecological green-space networks.

Another study by Jim and Chen (2009) showed that diverse landscape elements in cities are valued differently by residents. People are willing to pay a premium for attractive views. This study assessed the amenity value of two major types of natural landscape in Hong Kong: harbor and mountain. The study was based on 1474 transactions in 2005 and 2006 in 18 private housing estates in a residential district. The high-rise and high-density blocks were typical for middle-income housing in the city. The hedonic pricing method was employed to estimate the proportional share of various views and factors on transaction prices. Only harbor view was preferred and reflected in housing value. A broad harbor view could increase the value of an apartment by 2.97%, equivalent to US$ 15,173. Even a confined harbor view could lift price by 2.18% or US$ 11,137. On the contrary, a broad mountain view would depress apartment price by 6.7%, whereas a confined mountain view was statistically insignificant. Increasing distance between an apartment and a preferred natural landscape would lower transaction price. The negative perception of street view induced a price reduction by 3.7%. Building views were tolerated as an inevitable feature of the compact and vertical city. Quantifying the value of nature and scenic endowments in cities could inform policies and strategies on urban planning, development, nature conservation, and property appraisal.

A hedonic pricing method studies focused on the benefits of urban green spaces. In Portland, Oregon, 193 public parks ranging in size from 0.2 to 567.8 acres (0.081-229.96 ha), as a group, have a significant positive impact on the value of properties within a straight-line distance of 1500 ft (456 m) (Bolitzer and Netusil, 2000). Tyrväinen and Miettinen (2000) found that in the housing market of Salo (Finland), buyers have to pay 4.9% more to obtain a dwelling with a forest view. Proximity to the nearest forested park has a significant positive effect on house prices. An increase of 1 km distance from the forest is estimated to reduce the price of a dwelling by 5.9% meaning the farther is the distance the less is the price people are willing to pay. In the valuation of Boston's Big Dig Projects, the distance to parks has a negative correlation with property price. When the distance to the nearest park doubles, the property price was expected to decrease by 6% (Tajima, 2003). In another study of urban green spaces in the city of Castellón, Spain, the distance from a green area significantly affects housing price, but the size of the nearest green area or the views of a garden or a public park did not influence the prices (Bengochea-Morancho, 2003). Combined with water bodies, the effect of green spaces could be notably augmented. A garden bordering on water could attract a premium 28% higher than one without this attraction (Luttik, 2000).

Conclusion

Developers often found it difficult to link urban nature and environmental features to the quality of housing property market. For many real-estate developers, the implicit value of environmental attributes is seldom incorporated into the design and valuation of properties (Shi, 1994), thus curtailing their competitive edge in the burgeoning market. Hedonic pricing method is a powerful and appropriate research tool to assess the value of environmental benefits and resources, to estimate the worth of urban housing and to explore factors accounting for house pricing. Despite its wide applications in western countries, its use in Malaysia has yet to be developed. In the researches highlighted above the green view out of windows is strongly preferred by buyers implies that green spaces located within the residential grounds, with higher quality landscape design and management, with a higher degree of privacy and exclusiveness, and better security and safety, are more treasured by users (Van Herzele and Wiedemann, 2003). Green spaces which children can reach without crossing vehicular roads and can play safely with little supervision are particularly welcomed (Burgess et al., 1988). Thus the internal green spaces serve dual purposes, as recreational venues and as green scenery to provide pleasant view out of windows which could have a bearing on human physical and mental health ([Wilson, 1984] and [Ulrich, 1986]).

Compared with the external woods that cannot be used, the internal quasi-public green spaces within the neighborhood (Gobster, 2001) obviously have a competitive edge to contribute to housing price. It can be surmised that at least a room in the apartment with a view of internal green spaces would contribute to the selling price. More importantly, water bodies as a key landscape element designed to satisfy human affinity for the land—water interface. The water also serves to ameliorate air temperature extremes and improve human comfort. The fringes of water bodies are therefore well suited for public green spaces. Perception of water body quality might have influenced consumer behaviour. For the whole urban area, water view would increase price by 8.2% and green space view by 8.6%. Both green space view and the proximity to water bodies have notably enhanced residential housing price. Access to in situ quasi-public green spaces has secured an implicit value. Nearness to a wooded area which cannot be used by residents has not contributed to residential price, vividly portraying the consumers' pragmatic bent. It implies limited appreciation of the holistic and spill-over environmental benefits of natural areas. Thus green-space usability (direct and tangible benefit) could be more attractive than propinquity (indirect and less tangible benefits).

The roles played by green spaces and other environmental amenities on property price could be isolated and quantified. This research finding could provide an alternative and more holistic approach to analyze housing price structure and property value and to encompass environmental externalities. Developers could better understand a fundamental market determinant: how a home buyer decides on whether a dwelling is worthy of acquiring. It can literally bring the mindset of the consumer closer to the developer, build a bridge between the two parties, and use the feedback to rationalize key investment and pricing decisions.

The results in these study areas are comparable to the Malaysian property markets and tend to indicate similar buyer behaviour in reference to environmental elements. Naturalness is the principal physical attribute of greenspace in residential property areas appreciated by house buyers. Greenspace contribute to the improvement of quality of life, increased leisure time, and raised environmental awareness and expectation. Home buyers are willing to pay for what they prefer, desire or value. The locational preference was emphasized by ready access to usable green spaces, and availability of green and water views was stressed. This finding could inform Malaysian property developers concerning land selling and buying, land conversion, property development, urban nature conservation, and design of ecological green-space networks. To meet the increasingly affluent and discerning clientele, developers should offer good landscape and environment to lure buyers. Increasing attention should be devoted to beautifying residential grounds and bringing notable improvement in the quality and diversity of landscape designs. A green and pleasant outdoor environment has indeed become de rigueur in many residential estates, including both the mass and luxury markets.

Developers could apply the method to make an informed weighing of alternatives in land acquisition for residential development. The analysis could help judgment on marketability and potential profit margin. It could enlighten decision on whether to purchase a piece of expensive land situated in a densely urbanized area with limited room for green spaces, or a piece of cheaper rural land with similar green space rooms plus good external environment. The determination of sale prices of individual units could more accurately take into account people's preference and desire to have view or access to green spaces and other environmental amenities. Architectural and landscape design could be molded to improve the quantity and quality of such supplies to meet consumer demands and to raise the value of the development. The same environmental benefit, view of water body, could command greater value in new housing areas.